*Heads
Up
Helping!!*

Teaching Tips and Techniques for Working With ADD, ADHD, and Other Children With Challenges

Melinda L. Boring
MA-CCC/SLP

BP43

Printed in Victoria, Canada

National Library of Canada Cataloguing in Publication Data

Boring, Melinda L., 1960-
 Heads up helping! : teaching tips and techniques for working with ADD, ADHD and other children with challenges
Includes bibliographical references.
ISBN 1-55369-332-9
 1. Attention-deficit disorder children--Education.
 2. Special education. I. Boring, David Scott II. Title.
LC4704.B67 2002   371.93 C2002-901331-3

TRAFFORD

This book was published *on-demand* in cooperation with Trafford Publishing.
On-demand publishing is a unique process and service of making a book available for retail sale to the public taking advantage of on-demand manufacturing and Internet marketing.
On-demand publishing includes promotions, retail sales, manufacturing, order fulfilment, accounting and collecting royalties on behalf of the author.

Suite 6E, 2333 Government St., Victoria, B.C. V8T 4P4, CANADA
Phone   250-383-6864   Toll-free   1-888-232-4444 (Canada & US)
Fax   250-383-6804   E-mail   sales@trafford.com
Web site   www.trafford.com
TRAFFORD PUBLISHING IS A DIVISION OF TRAFFORD HOLDINGS LTD.
Trafford Catalogue #02-0145   www.trafford.com/robots/02-0145.html

10   9   8   7   6   5

ACKNOWLEDGMENTS

This book is dedicated to my children Josh, Beth, and Beckie. You have been my students and my teachers. You are in my heart forever.

I wish to thank the following people:

• My loving husband Scott, for his editing suggestions, support, patience, encouragement, and most of all for being with me on this journey.

• To Amy Weichel, for her excellent ideas and enthusiasm during the writing of this book. A true friend and valued colleague!

• To Darla Wojciechowski, for previewing this book, listening to the stories about my kids, and laughing with me.

• To all my co-workers at The Childhood League Center, for sharing ideas, showing dedication to children who learn differently and have special needs, and for encouraging me as I wrote this book.

• To Rodger Pyle of USA Martial Arts Training Center, for having the patience and willingness to learn how to work with my children's differences and for being an excellent instructor who both teaches and is teachable.

• To the Thursday Night Life Group at Linworth Road Community Church, for encouraging me during the hard times and for celebrating with me during the good times. Special thanks to Karl Werbovetz & Julie Lane-Werbovetz for the use of their empty apartment during my early days of writing.

• To Dick & Shari Wiseman and Barbara Brim of the Christian Parents Educational Fellowship for first encouraging me to become a workshop speaker and for later supporting the idea of starting my company, *Heads Up!*

• To the dedicated staff of Christian Home Educators of Ohio (CHEO), for inviting me to speak at their conferences and giving me the opportunity to teach and encourage many people.

• To the workshop attendees who urged me to write this book.

• To my parents, Ken & Marilyn Wiley, who showed me the power of the written word and believed in my ability to write this book.

Table of Contents

Heads Up! Helping

Preface

I have been writing this book for fourteen years. For thirteen years, the thoughts were forming and organizing themselves in my mind. During the past year, these thoughts finally emerged onto paper. It took me several years of homeschooling a child with differences before I felt like I might have learned a few things that would be helpful to other homeschoolers, and even longer before I was able to write them down.

Just about the time I realized that I wanted to share my ideas with others, I was asked to speak at the Northwest Ohio Christian Home Educators conference in Findlay, Ohio. I offered to do workshops on teaching special needs, since two of my children have Attention Deficit Hyperactivity Disorder, or ADHD.

When I went to that first conference as a speaker, the first workshop I was scheduled to present was "Helping the Distractible Child." Since most of my homeschooling friends had children with no apparent learning differences, I was amazed to see the workshop room fill with people who had come to hear me present on that topic.

I started my workshop that day by showing a photograph that is a snapshot of my family life. It captures my husband Scott, our three children, and myself on a ride during our vacation at Hershey Park in Pennsylvania. As the ride neared its end, the recorded tour voice instructed us to "Look at the camera and give us your best Hershey smile!" In the picture you can see my son Josh looking back over his shoulder. My husband has his arm around my youngest daughter, Beckie. She is looking at the camera as Scott points it out to her, but her body is turned completely sideways in her seat. My daughter Beth and I are looking straight into the camera and giving our best Hershey smiles.

When we walked out to the lobby and saw the photo, I asked Josh if he had heard the voice saying to look at the camera, and he said, "Yes, but there was something interesting back there that I wanted to look at!" That photograph is truly a picture of what life with Josh is like. He hears what is said, but has other ideas that compete for his attention and to this day I cannot predict his actions.

As I stood before the workshop attendees at that first conference and began to share stories from my family life, I prayed that God would use the time to give these devoted parents encouragement and ideas for helping their children. I did not have all the answers, and even the teaching tips I had to offer only worked some of the time with my own children. I offered what I could as a fellow parent doing the best she could for her children.

Homeschooling and parenting a child with differences has been the most challenging experience of my life. Having a son who is extremely distractible and hyperactive has sent me on a difficult and humbling journey not of my choosing. I love my son deeply, but we could not be more different from each other if we tried. As I continued to struggle over time to understand and help my son, it became increasingly apparent that my youngest daughter also had issues with hyperactivity and distractibility.

Sometimes my life reminds me of a walk through a carnival fun house, where perceptions are changed and it is difficult to predict what lies ahead. I never could have anticipated the lessons God has taught me through my three children. They have helped me to be a better teacher than I ever wanted to have to be! Through them, I have seen that I am not as patient as I thought I was. I have discovered strengths that I never had to tap into before I became a mother. I have also found the motivation to ask their forgiveness and continue the pursuit of raising and educating them with love.

Since that first workshop I presented at the homeschool conference several years ago, I have continued to explore and experiment with ways to teach children who learn differently. I continue to look for better materials and more effective ways to teach. I share my findings at workshops, and I share my heart's stories with those who are on difficult journeys of their own.

I am now in my ninth year of home schooling. I have been around the block a few more times – on my knees, it seems! I have experienced much joy as I have taught my children, and have had more laughter and satisfaction than in all my life prior to becoming a mother. I still don't have all the answers, and I continue to pray for wisdom and insight that will bless my family and others.

I hope that this book will give hope and encouragement to those who are struggling to raise and teach children who are somehow different. For those parents and teachers whose children do not have obvious differences, I hope they will gain greater understanding and compassion as a result of reading this book. Most of all, I hope that many children will benefit as adults read this book and learn new ways to connect with special and unique children.

Melinda

Please visit my website at www.headsupnow.com

Josh Boring, age 14

<u>Chapter 1 – The Journey Begins</u>

Entering Motherhood

When I gave birth to my first child, Joshua, I felt I had prepared as much as I possibly could in order to be a good mom. I had read parenting and child development books. I was conscientious about my health throughout the pregnancy. My husband, Scott, and I diligently attended Lamaze classes and punctually arrived for all doctor's appointments.

I worked with preschoolers in my job as a speech therapist, experience I was sure would help me when I had children of my own. When Josh arrived following a normal pregnancy and somewhat difficult delivery, I was ready for him. At least I thought so.

During Josh's first year of life, he was a very happy and contented baby. He didn't seem to mind going to the many activities my husband and I were involved in, happily letting others carry him around as his bright brown eyes watched all that was happening.

I was pleased when Josh met developmental milestones at the expected ages and seemed to be both healthy and intelligent. He walked and talked at about age one year, and I provided him with educational toys and lots of books, which we happily shared each day.

I was somewhat disappointed when Josh gave up napping in the morning, and I noticed that he did not sleep as long at night as others his age. He was also very physically active, which was true of many little boys I knew so that was not a cause for concern.

When Josh was fifteen months old, his sister Beth was born. Josh displayed only delight and amusement at her arrival. He watched with interest and laughter as Beth developed and responded to his attention and attempts to entertain her. He was gentle and patient with Beth, and didn't show the slightest sign of jealousy.

Josh continued his relentless exploration of the world, and it was when he was about a year and a half old that I first became concerned that Josh's enthusiasm might endanger him and signify something more than childish curiosity.

I knew Josh could understand a great deal of what was said to him. I had his hearing screened numerous times and it was always within normal limits. Yet I was finding that often I had to repeat what I was saying to Josh several times before he responded. Particularly if I was not right next to him, he acted as though he didn't even hear me. This led to much frustration for me, because I was sure Josh knew what I was saying and comprehended it perfectly.

My first attempt to correct this behavior in Josh was to make sure I was consistent in following through with any directions I gave him. I read books about strong-willed children, and wanted to help Josh before he developed bad habits such as ignoring people when they talked to him. My husband likewise strove to be consistent in expecting Josh to respectfully respond to us when we spoke to him.

After a period of time during which we attempted to teach Josh the importance of listening and responding to others, I noticed that Josh actually was beginning to respond more frequently. His response, however, was often "huh?" or "what?" After another hearing test that confirmed that his hearing was fine in both ears, my speech therapist training entered the mix.

I began to wonder if Josh had difficulty processing other's speech. When auditory processing is an issue, a child often needs additional time to process and respond to what has been said. Children with normal hearing may say "what?" even though they heard the speaker, just to gain the extra time they need to process information or because it helps them to hear the information repeated. So I began working in earnest on Josh's listening and processing skills, applying every therapy technique I had learned.

The Preschool Years

During the preschool years, I began noticing other characteristics that set Josh apart from others his age. He did not seem to learn from experience. He engaged in certain behaviors such as flipping the switches on his Daddy's stereo repeatedly, even though I consistently stopped him and redirected him to acceptable activities. Consequences did not seem to phase him much, and only affected him as they were occurring with no generalization beyond that moment.

Josh's activity level only increased as his motor skills developed and allowed him access to more areas. He was an accomplished climber, and was indiscriminate about what he climbed. He appeared fearless as he attempted to scale any object that represented a challenge or a means to a desired object. I could not merely put objects up out of his reach, they needed to be placed out of his sight when he was not watching or he would try to figure out a way to get to them.

The entire family is affected when a child has special needs, and this was certainly the case for our family. For two summers we could not leave the front door to our house open to allow breezes to come through our screen door because Josh had quickly learned how to unlock the door and escape to the great outdoors.

We tried placing a latch high up on the screen door so that Josh would be unable to reach it. Josh noticed the "problem" and stared intently at the new apparatus for a few minutes. It took him less than 24 hours to figure out if he climbed on top of the couch, leaned *waaay* over and stretched, he could undo the latch. Hello, freedom! Hello, world!

Fans? Only if an adult stood guard to keep Josh's fingers and toys away from the spinning fan blades. Josh was likewise unaware of the dangers of leaving the house without my knowledge, or of the perils of traffic passing by our house. It was a couple of hot, stuffy summers spent trying to keep Josh safe.

Josh really seemed to want to please, and did not appear to be obstinate or defiant. Sometimes he would be so absorbed in his play that when I came up next to him and spoke he appeared startled to see me there. I became more and more convinced that what I was seeing with Josh was not a matter of his being strong-willed or having a disagreeable attitude. I just couldn't figure out what *was* going on with him.

When I took Josh to preschool programs at parks or story times at the library, he seemed to enjoy them and was excited to attend. At the same time, actually being in a group seemed to over-excite and overwhelm him. Josh wanted to play with the other children, but could not figure out how to join in appropriately; rather, he tended to play alongside others or intrude on them, but not interact directly with them.

When outdoors or in a large open area, Josh's excitement manifested in greatly increased physical activity and decreased ability to control his bodily movements, listen to others, and follow directions. He needed to run and jump, but often did not notice obstacles or watch where he was going. The bumps and falls left him decorated with bruises.

In smaller or crowded areas such as the library story room, Josh pressed into my side or remained on my lap. He could observe, but did not participate despite encouragement and support from me. He remembered all that happened during the activities, but talked about them later instead of when they were actually happening.

The few times Josh did leave my lap during story times were for his favorite activity- flannel board stories. Unfortunately, he always positioned himself directly in front of the flannel board and had to be asked to sit down so others could see the story, too. Josh struggled to restrain himself from moving back to his preferred position for the best possible view of the story, and he really longed to move the flannel pieces around and make up his own story. Our kind librarian allowed Josh to stand by her side while she told the stories, and let him see and handle the flannel board pieces when story time was over.

Advice and Isolation

Throughout the preschool years, I frequently received unsolicited advice from strangers as well as friends and relatives. When Josh did something odd or totally missed nonverbal cues, people would give me a look that varied from disgust to pity. Some told me "All that kid needs is a good swat!" while others lectured me on their formula for parenting success. A quick review told us that if we followed this course, we would be spanking Josh almost continually.

I needed help, but often people shared techniques I had already tried or implemented. Most people did not want to hear how difficult it was to parent a child like Josh. It seemed they only wanted me to somehow "fix" him so he would act like others his age and wouldn't bother and annoy them. I had no idea how to change Josh into someone fundamentally different than whom he was, and was not sure I wanted to in any case. I had a feeling Josh would never be like most kids his age.

I attended a "Mom's Time Out" program at a church once. This was a time for mothers to hear a speaker on a topic related to mothering, have refreshments, and visit with other mothers. I looked forward to it and hoped to find some much needed support to bolster my diminishing confidence in my mothering skills.

Josh was in the two-year-olds' room and Beth was next door in the one-year-olds' room. It was a pleasant morning, and at the conclusion of the program I headed toward the childcare area to pick up my children. I was happy that my name had not been written up on the board during the morning, since that was the signal used to indicate that my children needed me immediately.

As I stepped into the childcare hallway, a woman I had never seen before confronted me with "Are you Joshua's Mom?" When I acknowledged that I was, she began a litany of his morning's activities, telling me that among other things he had given one of the teachers a black eye.

I was shocked, because although Josh was clumsy and bumped into things frequently, I had never seen him act deliberately aggressive or disrespectful to anyone. As she continued to expound on Josh's behavior in animated detail, I excused myself in order to get to him.

I was confused at this apparent new behavior in my son, and I was concerned that I had not been summoned immediately when the trouble occurred. Before I made it to his room, another unfamiliar woman saw my nametag and inquired if I was Josh's mom. I again acknowledged that I was and this new person began to tell me how Josh had given a teacher a black eye and did not respond when the adults called to him from across the room.

At this point, I became concerned for Josh, because I knew he could not screen out background noises to hear directions given from across a room. I feared he would be misunderstood and would be confused by the caretaker's reactions to him. I again excused myself as the second woman began complaining in great detail about my son's behavior. I was anxious to get to Josh.

I now felt like I was performing a rescue operation as I finally made it to the doorway of the two-year-olds' room to regain my son. My heart broke as I saw him sitting in a chair, physically restrained by an adult who was scolding him with "You didn't listen so now you have to sit here until your mom comes." Josh looked incredibly sad and bewildered. He had no idea what was expected of him, he was in an unfamiliar place with new people, and he hated being confined and not allowed to move.

How I wished they had asked for me to come sooner. I never found out how long he had been sitting there. All I could think about was getting Josh out of there, and when I saw how many children were in the room and how noisy it was, I realized that Josh could not have tuned in to any teacher who called to him from across the room. It was a set-up for failure for him, even though he was only two years of age.

When I quickly informed a helper that I was there to pick Josh up, she replied with "Oh. I need to talk to you." This was now the third person to complain to me about my son and describe the difficulties he had caused the workers. By now I was sorry I had even come to the program. Every ounce of encouragement I had gained from the morning dissolved, as I scooped my son into my arms. I felt more isolated than ever, and it grieved me that my son had such a rough time when I had hoped he might have fun with others his age.

With Josh firmly in my arms he began to relax, and I asked the childcare worker why I had not been contacted since the workers were obviously having so much trouble with my son during the meeting. I had watched the message board closely, and my name had never been on it.

I also wanted to know exactly what had transpired up to the time Josh gave the teacher a black eye. Josh was clearly distressed, and just held on to me with both hands clutching my shirt as we stood there. As I asked questions to elicit information I finally heard the actual details of what had taken place.

I was told that the children were gathered in a circle to sing and play games. For one of the games the children jumped up and down to music. Josh joined in, but jumped off the beat and his head bumped the cheekbone of the adult next to him. There was some soreness but it was not a black eye. There had been no deliberate intent to injure. Josh lacked rhythm and had shown over-exuberance, but had not been aggressive or physically violent.

Unfortunately, others had been saying that Josh had given a teacher a black eye, which made me wonder if he was already being labeled as a kind of troublemaker.

I knew Josh would never deliberately hurt anyone, but I didn't know if I would be able to convince others of that.

I was relieved that Josh had not hurt anyone on purpose, and Josh and I moved on to the next room to pick up his sister. I was greeted warmly and told how sweet and wonderful Beth was throughout the morning.

It was good to hear something encouraging about one of my children, though by then I was emotionally spent. The reception I received when I went to pick Josh up from the childcare room and the concern over what Josh's future experiences there might be kept me from going back to that program. The emotional toll and the risk to Josh's sense of well-being were too high.

Going to church on Sunday mornings was another challenging activity for us. I would take Josh to Sunday School, explain to the teacher what I knew about helping Josh with his difficulties in group settings, and then head for the worship service. Often this was the only hour I had each week to be with other adults without having my children with me.

Even so, I wondered at times if it was worth it, because when I went to pick Josh up from his class I was typically greeted with "I need to talk to you about Josh." There was never much variation to those conversations. I typically heard descriptions of the various ways that Josh showed he was not paying attention and not sitting still or how different or difficult he was. Often I heard detailed descriptions of specific episodes that took place. I did not hear anything that was unusual for Josh, but it was disheartening to be told about it repeatedly and as if I did not realize or care deeply about Josh and his struggles.

Life at Home

When Josh was five years old and Beth was four years old, their sister Rebecca was born. Beckie was a responsive, affectionate baby with an easy-going nature. Josh was endearingly careful and attentive with both of his younger sisters. He was gentle with the baby, and strove to entertain and comfort her. Josh encouraged Beth to try new tasks and applauded her successes.

I wished others could see some of the positive characteristics we saw in Josh at home, but the agitation that he experienced in any group setting only emphasized his struggles and differences. Only the immediate family got to see the sweetest aspects of Josh, and I toyed with the idea of videotaping him so others could see what I saw in this wonderful, yet challenging boy.

The spring before Josh was to start kindergarten, I retested his language and processing skills to see if the extra work on his listening skills had helped. I was thrilled to see that Josh was at or above age-level in all areas, but now I was faced with a dilemma.

Josh still had trouble following directions, especially in a group setting. He became agitated when asked to sit still and was willing but unable to comply. He seemed easily distracted by sights, sounds, and even odors that most people didn't even notice. He was impulsive in his actions and was drawn to the most engaging stimulus of the moment. Children who were quietly doing tasks were not the strongest stimuli for Josh, so he often needed redirection and reminders of what he should be doing.

I was concerned that Josh would not do well in a classroom setting. I envisioned him being constantly corrected by weary teachers and, eventually, by other classmates. I did not want to see Josh having to endure frequent sessions in "time out" or be isolated for not following directions, distracting other children, or blurting out answers.

Having worked in the schools, I knew from experience that teachers liked some children more easily than others. Josh was not going to be easy to teach, and I knew he would need a great deal of individual attention. His creativity and unusual ideas often sent him in different directions than any teacher could anticipate. It would take a rare and compassionate teacher to see my son positively in this light.

I remained convinced that my son was bright in some ways, and I also knew that this was not readily apparent to others. This was especially true when Josh was seen in a group setting. I did not want Josh growing up believing he was inherently inferior to others. I did not want him negatively mislabeled because he was different than most his age. I wasn't sure exactly what was causing the differences with Josh, but I was committed to helping him succeed in every way he could.

My husband and I discussed Josh for hours, determining to help him and consider all options for his education. I've already reviewed some of our concerns about public schools and Josh's difficulties when in group settings. We also considered private schools, but eventually concluded that the same issues applied. Private tutoring was cost prohibitive, and we knew very little about home schooling. There were no easy answers and we realized that our decision would have a monumental impact on our lives.

Josh Boring, age 14

Chapter 2 – Let the Formal Education Begin!

Getting Started

I was initially resistant to the idea of home schooling. I have a degree in education, and I always did very well in school. As a parent, I looked forward to being a room mother and bringing cookies to my children's classes. I planned to be very involved with my children's education, accompanying them on field trips, and volunteering in the classroom. But I had to admit that Josh was a very different kind of student than I had been, and his way of learning was not compatible with a typical classroom setting. I reluctantly conceded that home schooling was our best option.

I attended a state homeschool convention three months before Josh would start kindergarten. I was amazed and overwhelmed at the magnitude of curriculum and educational supplies in the vendor area. Deciding which materials to use was going to be much more difficult than I had anticipated.

I knew I needed to use a "hands-on" approach as much as possible, because Josh seemed to learn more easily when he could see and touch materials. I began looking and asking as many questions as I could think of at the time. I talked to others to find out about materials that they had used, and I picked up many catalogs to look for additional materials as needed.

In addition to supplies for Josh, I bought a few books on learning differences for myself as well. As with every major planned event in my life, I attempted to prepare thoroughly. I read books on home schooling and talked to others about the educational choices they had made for their children. The few people I knew who had children with issues similar to Josh's issues seemed very relieved to send them to school, and I understood their decision to do so. I did not know anyone who was homeschooling a child with differences or special needs of any kind.

I enrolled Josh in a home school support group so he could take group classes one morning each week and attend monthly field trips. I hoped the group classes would be a good experience for Josh since the class size was limited to 15 students. Also, many of the other students were from our church, so the familiarity might help. In addition, he would get experience with teachers other than myself, and could become friends with the other children.

Armed with solid curriculum and motherly devotion, I began to teach at home in earnest. I wrote detailed lesson plans. I was organized and prepared for each subject, and had an area of our home set aside for school activities. I taught as I had been taught, and as my college education had trained me to teach. I immersed myself in the task of educating my children.

Our Typical School Day

Josh was a bright student, quick to pick up on new concepts and ideas. His sister, Beth, was also an eager student and I quickly abandoned the idea of just teaching her preschool skills and allowed her to do the same kindergarten work as her brother. I taught them together and carefully explained the work I wanted them to do.

Josh was able to verbalize his understanding of assignments with ease. He would then proceed to tell me how he would like to do them differently, and always had many reasons and ideas to change the assignment from its original form. He could easily spend forty minutes writing out an assignment that he could answer orally or by pointing in two minutes.

For example, if the math page had directions to draw a line from the number six to the pictures showing groups of six, Josh could quickly point out which groups that would include. But when given a pencil and told to complete the page, he would draw elaborate pictures of looping fences with bees sitting on them. This is the way he connected the number and group of objects, rather than just drawing a straight line and finishing the page. Each pictured group would get a different, but equally detailed drawing.

Once an adult showed Josh how to slightly change a basic drawing to make a "flip book" so that as the pages on a pad were rapidly flipped it would look as if the pictures were animated. Josh was fascinated and immediately got to work on his own flipbook. Within twenty minutes he had completed one book and had ideas for many more.

This display of creativity was not limited to any certain subject, but was evident in every area of schoolwork involving paper and pencil tasks. We started calling Josh by the nickname "Ford," because he "always had a better idea." He was also persistent in sharing his views.

My friends who started home schooling for kindergarten the same year I did were able to finish the schoolwork in two or two and a half hours each day. Due to Josh's need for frequent breaks and his creative prolongation of even the simplest assignments, it was taking us eight or nine hours each day.

While waiting for Josh to finish his work, Beth would frequently ask me "What's next?" and be eager to do more schoolwork. Often she had to wait for Josh to finish a task so that I would not have to teach everything at two different times throughout the day.

So Many Distractions

When I started home schooling my children, I had them sit at desks. I had one room where all the school supplies were kept and we started work at the same time each morning. The lessons were prepared in advance and I took a very organized approach to presenting material. I quickly learned that I needed to make some additional adjustments to try and minimize the effects of Josh's distractibility.

Although Beckie was generally a content baby, her slightest vocalization distracted Josh. Likewise for traffic noises, household appliance motors, or the scrape of a chair moving on the floor. These types of noises I automatically tuned out and would be unaware of until Josh pointed them out to me. He seemed unable to block out the background noises in order to concentrate on the significant sounds he was supposed to attend to at the time.

Josh also displayed an increased sensitivity to smell. When I'd lean over his shoulder to explain the directions on a workbook page, Josh would comment about the smell of coffee or chewing gum on my breath. If I were wearing cologne or scented lotion, he'd wrinkle up his nose. Even odors that were pleasurable to Josh were sources of distraction, but most smells seemed aversive to him.

We also were challenged by Josh's responses to visual distractions. When Josh perceived movement, even peripheral movement, he had to look to find the source. When I went to attend to one of his sisters, his eyes followed every movement I made. When his sister dropped her pencil and bent down to pick it up, Josh watched. He seemed unable to force himself to look at any book or object for any length of time beyond half a minute. His head moved as if on a swivel base, as though he was constantly scanning the environment with his eyes.

Another area of distraction for Josh was his own internal state. If he was the slightest bit hungry or thirsty, he had significant difficulty concentrating. If his clothing felt too tight or too loose to him, it distracted him. Once he was aware of the sensation, he was unable to ignore or delay responding to it.

Often, ideas of drawings or creations he wanted to make filled his mind and he felt compelled to tell me about them despite what I was trying to accomplish academically at the moment. Although we severely limited video and television viewing, Josh was able to remember and describe shows he had seen even weeks before. Once a thought or memory occurred to him, he appeared unable to stop thinking and talking about it despite my prompts to complete his schoolwork first.

If I left the room to attend to the baby or answer the phone, I'd often return a few minutes later to find Josh totally absorbed with his latest Lego invention or drawing. When I asked why he hadn't completed his work, he often replied with "I had this idea…" and would proceed to describe his idea to me in detail.

His ideas were often very imaginative, and although I was glad for his creativity, I was not happy that it was seriously interfering with his ability to complete schoolwork. Josh claimed that he wanted to do a good job on his schoolwork, but he did not demonstrate that desire to me in ways that were easily recognizable.

Disorganization

Josh's kindergarten year was a time of great frustration to me. I felt guilty because he required a disproportionate amount of my time and I worried that my daughters weren't getting as much attention from me as they should. Schoolwork lasted most of the day, leaving little time for any housework, personal development, or relaxation. Although I felt chronically exhausted and frequently discouraged, I was still convinced that Josh was learning in the best atmosphere we could provide.

Our house often looked disheveled. Josh's projects spread out to cover all available surface area. I regularly insisted on cleaning up and limiting the clutter of toys, projects, and clothes to designated containers. Even so, when Josh played or worked he scattered everything out so he could view it all at once, and was always reluctant to put things away.

Josh did not organize his belongings in any recognizable way, and resisted my organizing methods. He put things away only with great reluctance and much supervision. His disorganization frequently resulted in an inability to find needed or desired objects in a timely manner.

Josh's disorganization with schoolwork took the form of misplaced pencils and other supplies, piles of artwork mixed with workbooks and written assignments, and a desk so stuffed full of toys and school supplies that a family of mice could have lived quite comfortably in the back and gone undetected for some time. Actually, Josh would have immediately heard and smelled any mice, but it would have taken him a significant amount of time to determine their precise location!

Group Classes

Josh's experience with home school group classes was consistent with the behaviors I'd seen him display in other group settings. I worked closely with his teachers for art, music, creative writing, and physical education.

The teachers were kind and caring, and tried to help Josh as best they could while teaching fourteen other children.

Josh had extreme difficulty waiting his turn when he needed help or had something to say. His teachers and I patiently repeated the acceptable behaviors for Josh to practice in the classroom. He could state the rules when asked, but continued to struggle when he actually had to comply.

Josh absolutely loved the art class, which was not surprising considering his creative tendencies. Unfortunately, he often did not finish his art projects due to a combination of getting distracted by the other students' activities and his complex ideas for artistic endeavors. The portions of projects he did complete were beautifully detailed and again revealed Josh's creativity. Josh would corner even the most nominally interested person so he could tell him or her about his artwork and what it would have looked like if he'd been able to finish his project.

Music class bombarded Josh with multiple sights and sounds. At times he would just sit and observe the class, alertly scanning the room. Sometimes he kept his hands over his ears to block out the excess noise. His intent was to lessen the overwhelming tidal wave of sensory impulses that too much auditory stimulation brought about, but he probably appeared rude and disinterested. He rarely sang with his group, although he enjoyed music and sang at times when he was at home. He seemed unable to cope with the massive amount of sensory information in addition to attempting to follow the teacher's instructions.

Creative writing class presented the usual challenges when Josh was given a paper and pencil task. He often doodled on his paper or writing folder, depicting animated stories through his drawings. When it came to written words, however, Josh rarely produced more than a paragraph even with adult prompting.

An exception to this was when Josh dictated a story for an adult to write down. At those times, Josh showed a facility for the use of language and grammar that was most impressive. I was puzzled as to why he seemed unable to write down his ideas independently, especially since he was never short of ideas.

Physical education class was the toughest of all, though not for reasons relating to Josh's physical abilities. Josh was sturdy and healthy, and had energy to spare. But when faced with a group of shouting children engaging in fast-paced activities, Josh withdrew to a position under a table in the gym room and observed the class activities from that location.

His slowness at processing oral directions and his hypersensitivity to sound was only exacerbated by the noise and poor acoustics of the room. He did not know what he was supposed to be doing, what others were doing, and where he needed to be for the games and exercises. So he coped by withdrawing to what must have seemed to him to be a safer location under the table.

No amount of coaxing by the teacher or myself could persuade Josh to join in the activities. He ventured out for short periods of time, but always retreated back to his safe spot when he felt confused or overwhelmed. After observing his class for a while, Josh sometimes could figure out the rules for the games and then he would emerge from under the table and join in the play.

Josh participated in field trips with his usual enthusiasm. The chaos of a large group in a new setting seemed to agitate Josh into constant motion, but he still seemed able to take in the educational aspects at least part of the time. I had to stay constantly by his side to prevent him from impulsively grabbing objects that were off limits for touching, and to keep him from darting off to potentially dangerous areas. Fortunately, my other two children were not prone to stray far from my side and other mothers on the field trip helped with them.

Josh struggled socially with people of all ages, but especially with those his own age. His propensity to blurt things out, his impulsiveness, and his lack of skill in noticing nonverbal cues such as facial expression all led to varying degrees of rejection. Josh was genuinely bewildered when overt rejection occurred, but it was not in keeping with his temperament to dwell on the unpleasantness for long.

All of these observations reinforced our conviction that Josh marched to the beat of a different drummer. In fact, Josh seemed to have an entirely different orchestra. Yet we were still searching for an explanation for what made Josh so different from most other kids.

Josh Boring, age 14

Chapter 3 – The Search For Understanding

I desperately searched the library for resources that could help me understand why my son acted and reacted in the ways he did. Still strongly believing Josh was intelligent as well as creative, I checked out books on "The Gifted Child". To my dismay, Josh had several of the negative characteristics of a gifted child but was not exhibiting the positive, classic characteristics. He also did not fit the profiles for being dyslexic or having the other learning disabilities I read about.

I knew he had not been exposed to harmful substances prenatally, and I was careful to provide him with healthy nutrition. I restricted his consumption of sugar, caffeine, and other questionable substances. He'd had regular medical care since his birth. He did not sleep as much as I would have liked him to, but he appeared well rested and healthy. He had been provided with educational materials, love, and deep affection since infancy. I was truly at a loss as to what could be causing Josh to have such difficulties in areas others easily navigated with no special accommodations.

Eureka!

I cannot remember exactly when, or what source I was reading at the time of my revelation about Josh. I only know that at some time during his kindergarten year I came across some material that described attention deficit hyperactivity disorder (ADD/ADHD). There was a list of characteristics, and the criteria required that a certain number of those characteristics be present over a period of time and by a certain age in order for the diagnosis to be made.

At that time, two types of attention deficit disorder were described. It could occur with (ADHD) or without (ADD) hyperactivity. Josh significantly exceeded the minimum number of characteristics described for the diagnosis of attention deficit hyperactivity disorder. In fact, he was over-qualified!

I was relieved to at last have an idea of what was going on with my son. The three classic symptoms of inattention, disorganization, and impulsivity were exactly what I had been seeing in Josh for years. I began the process of educating myself on the topic of attention deficit hyperactivity disorder. I was hopeful and optimistic that knowing about ADHD would help me find solutions to the many obstacles Josh was facing.

The more I read about attention deficit disorder, the more I understood about Josh and his ways of responding. I came to understand ADHD as a neurologically based disorder, one that Josh had most likely been born with and would probably have his entire life. I learned about the brain and how it functions, and this helped me to realize why Josh had difficulty applying concepts he clearly understood and could verbalize in his calmer moments.

Educating myself about ADHD also reassured me that there were people interested in learning about the disorder and knowledgeable individuals who were willing to share their expertise with others. I found books and magazine articles, and began the formidable task of learning all I could on the subject of ADHD. My son, my family, and my very life had been affected by ADHD and its manifestations. I desperately hoped that learning about this disorder would help me be a better parent and lead to more effective ways of helping Josh.

Theories and Treatments

In my search for information, I found that there were many theories regarding the cause and treatment of ADHD. It became apparent that individuals often felt very strongly about their stated positions, and voiced their opinions in no uncertain terms. I was determined to learn about the various points of view, and then discern which seemed to make the most sense in regards to Josh and my family.

I read information from a variety of sources, starting with the view that ADHD symptoms are actually dietary reactions to certain substances. I continued my study with some authors who viewed ADHD as entirely behavioral in nature, and reviewed the various treatments recommended. I read information by those claiming that there was no such thing as attention deficit disorder, with blame for the symptoms being attributed to sinful behavior on the child's part or poor parenting skills by the mother and/or father. I read testimonials from parents who declared their child's life had been vastly improved by using medication. I read information by parents who resisted the use of medication or who had their child try it and vowed never to "drug" their child again.

Clearly, even now there would be no easy answers. I knew I was seeing a real disorder in Josh, but it would take much prayer and discernment to know how to proceed. I did not find any one approach that seemed like the perfect fit for Josh or our family. I sifted through the vast amount of information I had gathered and carefully selected which aspects I was willing to consider trying with Josh.

I was also willing to discard any idea or strategy that did not seem to be a good fit for Josh. I explained to him that we were going to try some different things to see if they would help him in areas that were hard for him. I counted on him to tell me how he perceived them and what effect they had on him. I also carefully observed Josh as each new strategy was introduced, to see if I noticed any differences as well.

The Label Controversy

In my relief at finally having a name for what I had struggled to identify for so long, I shared my findings perhaps too freely with others. I discovered the same controversy among my acquaintances as I had found in literature about ADHD. There were many strongly held viewpoints as to the cause and treatment of ADHD.

Some people tried to tell me "All boys are like that." Others claimed to know someone who had outgrown their symptoms as they matured, or who had been misdiagnosed. Still others suggested that all people have the symptoms of ADD. The strongest feelings expressed seemed to be regarding the use of medication to treat ADHD. Those who opposed the use of medication were the most vehement of all who expressed their opinions.

During this period of time, I watched Josh in the home school gym class as he was once again struggling to participate in the group activity. His awkward attempts to cope with the noise and crowding of his classmates caused him to stand out and be noticed. Along with a few other adults, I had arrived before the class was finished and stood off to the side with other mothers as we observed the class.

I noticed the woman next to me, who was staring at Josh with a perplexed expression on her face. I explained that I was Josh's mother, and that he had ADHD. I briefly described how difficult it was for him to attend to a teacher's voice when there was a lot of competing noise and activity occurring at the same time. This mother's response was to tell me that she just hated to see children labeled, especially at such a young age. I politely responded that I agreed, and that one of the reasons I had Josh officially diagnosed was to put an end to having him **mis**labeled – as defiant, disobedient, stubborn, stupid, noncompliant, and more.

A label can be useful, if it helps to increase understanding and direct appropriate treatment. It can also prevent other labels from being inaccurately applied to the child. Knowing that there was a term for what I observed in Josh gave me ideas to investigate, others to talk to, and a sense that perhaps this conglomeration of symptoms could be managed successfully.

Of course all children are unique individuals, even those who share the same diagnoses. As in the selection of curriculum for Josh, I had to sift through information on ADHD to determine which descriptions were accurate for Josh and which ones were not. I had to push ahead, knowing that whatever I decided to do, some people would disapprove while others would be in hearty agreement.

Being an Advocate

I became an advocate for Josh, preemptively speaking to any adult who would be working with him or teaching him in any capacity. I learned to describe ADHD as it applied to Josh, and to demonstrate teaching strategies and techniques that worked best for him. I wanted others to know the truth about Josh, and not judge him harshly for his obvious differences without understanding the basis for those struggles. I developed the habit of interviewing anyone who would be working directly with Josh prior to enrolling him in any sports activities or classes. Most instructors were receptive to hearing my expectations for Josh in a group setting.

I found that many people had no experience working with a child who learns in unique ways, and most of them seemed glad that I took the time to make the experience more successful for Josh as well as the instructor. I knew that it would not take long for any teacher to realize that Josh was unusual, and I wanted them to know how best to respond to him. I didn't want to wait until there was frustration and misunderstanding for both Josh and the teacher. Although I never had all the answers for how to work with Josh, I shared the tips that seemed to work at least some of the time. Most instructors willingly entered into a partnership with me, working together to find methods that worked for Josh.

As I gained understanding about what was going on in my son, I began to have some hope that there were ways to compensate for what I was observing. The frustrating part was that it seemed that as soon as I "got a grip" on one situation, another would develop, and I would have to start all over again. I discovered that distractibility has many forms!

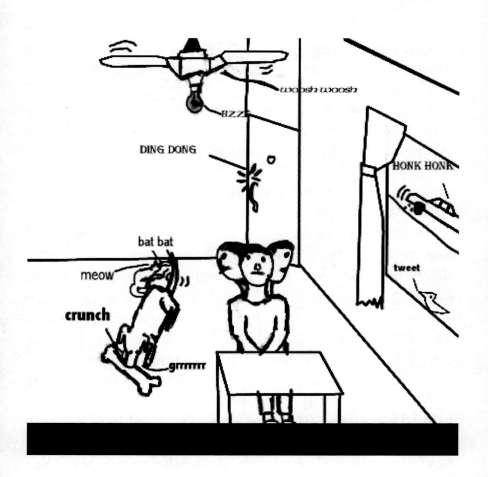

Chapter 4 – Auditory Distractibility

Auditory distractibility is often apparent even in very young children. Some children seem to have such good hearing sensitivity that they can hear even soft sounds at a distance. They seem highly tuned in to what they hear, although it is often selective and they tune in to a particular sound to the exclusion of all other sounds. Josh is an example of a child who has always been exceptionally alert to noises of all types.

"Did You Hear That?"

"An airplane, an airplane!" Josh shouted excitedly, interrupting our reading lesson yet again. I paused and concentrated, then faintly heard the engine noise of a distant airplane. We were inside the house with all of the windows and doors closed, yet Josh noticed a sound that was barely audible to me even when I strained to hear it. As quiet as our neighborhood typically was, it was not quiet enough to eliminate auditory distractions for Josh.

Often I would be in the midst of teaching when Josh would suddenly ask, "What was that?". Josh had a need to identify every sound he heard – and he seemed to hear sounds that most people were unaware of unless they were concentrating intently on hearing them. Not only did Josh hear the sounds, he felt the need to identify their source immediately and often imitated the sounds he heard.

I had to laugh one day when I heard a vaguely familiar noise and realized Josh was imitating the sounds of our neighbor's leaf blower! He could also make a close approximation of a vacuum cleaner noise, although such loud noises bothered him and he often covered his ears in the presence of loud sounds. By imitating noises and drawing my attention to even the softest of sounds, Josh demonstrated that he was highly attuned to some auditory stimuli even from a young age.

Josh has always been bothered by loud noises. He would watch the airplanes overhead with fascination, but his hands would remain firmly clamped over his ears the entire time.   Parades were highly stimulating and enjoyable for Josh, but the bands were too loud for his sensitive ears.   He would usually cover his ears and retreat several feet back from the band, where hopefully the hard-working musicians could not see Josh with his ears covered! He enjoyed the music, just not the volume level.

Once we went to a demolition derby exhibition at a fair, and we had to wad up tissue for Josh to put in his ears so he could tolerate the noise. He was enthusiastic about watching the exhibition, but was becoming increasingly agitated by the noise level. I offered to leave with him, but he was reluctant to miss the show so we tried the tissue in the ears and it made the noise bearable for him. We also had selected seats near the back of the arena, which turned out to be a good idea for helping to slightly lower the noise level.

When my daughter, Beckie, was seven years old she described her auditory distractibility for me in an unforgettable word picture. We had been working together on her schoolwork, and she was becoming increasingly frustrated by her difficulty in concentrating on her work. "You know what the problem is, Mom?" she asked me. "My ears are like the cat's." I pondered this statement, with visions of my daughter equipped with fuzzy and pointed ears running through my mind. Fortunately, Beckie went on to explain her statement. "I hear things that other people don't hear, just like our cat does. I hear the dishwasher. I hear Josh walking upstairs even when I'm downstairs and supposed to be doing my work. I hear Beth sharpening her pencil upstairs in her room. And it keeps me from being able to concentrate on my schoolwork."

Beckie's story is a perfect example of what life is like for those with auditory distractibility. They are unable to consistently screen out insignificant or background noises. Most people are not even aware of these noises, much less distracted by them. But for those with auditory distractibility, it can be nearly incapacitating when it comes to concentrating and accomplishing some tasks.

Auditory Distractibility in Adults

As an adult, I am aware of my own struggles with auditory distractibility. In my work as a speech therapist, it has been an asset to hear even the slightest nuance and differences between speech sounds. I am unable, however, to listen and attend to more than one sound at a time. When I am reading, writing, trying a new recipe, or any other task requiring my concentration I do best in quiet areas. Multiple sounds distract me.

When I am doing speech therapy, I concentrate intensely on the children's pronunciation of sounds. I have to attend and hear even the slightest distortions in order to help the children attain clear speech. The scrutiny is necessary, and requires my focused attention. The children I work with enjoy practicing their speech sounds while playing card games with me, because they almost always win. I concentrate so exclusively on their speech pronunciation that I don't closely attend to the game itself. I do my best work when I can concentrate on one thing at a time.

At home, my children have learned that they need to talk to me in turns rather than all at once. At times they come rushing up to me, all talking at the same time. I honestly cannot process that level of auditory bombardment. I described for them how I could only listen and respond to one voice at a time, and they have realized that they must wait, then each will be heard in turn. This is actually more practical in the long run than having to repeat what they've said because I couldn't process three voices talking to me at once. I explained to them that when more than one person talks to me at the same time, my brain says "duuuuuuuuh…." until only one voice is heard. They seemed to understand this!

If your child is not aware of her responses to distraction, try pointing out your observations and the behaviors you notice when your child loses focus on the task at hand. For example, you might say something such as "I notice that every time you hear a sound you look around to see where it's coming from." Maybe your child notices when the dishwasher cycle changes, or when a sibling quietly sighs. As you discuss your observations with your child, she may become more aware of the types of distractions that are difficult for her to ignore and together you can think of possible strategies to help in those areas.

Strategies

Children with auditory distractibility need the quietest work area possible. Structure the work area so that noises from outside the home are minimized. Keep in mind that many items within the home that frequently generate background noise may not be noticeable to you but could be distracting to your child. Doors between rooms may need to be shut to decrease the audibility of some sounds. A ticking clock, the refrigerator motor, and the furnace turning on may all be sources of auditory distraction to a child with difficulties in this area.

In our home, Beth enjoys listening to music and will often have music playing while she does her chores and other activities. Unfortunately, although Josh likes music he is not able to concentrate on his schoolwork when he hears music playing. It does not matter what room Beth is in, Josh can hear when she has music on and he is distracted by it. Rather than denying Beth the enjoyment she receives from hearing music, we provided her with a personal cassette/radio with headphones. This way, she can continue to listen to music and Josh does not hear it and become distracted.

In addition to making changes in the physical location for schoolwork, some children find it helpful to wear headphones, earmuffs, or foam earplugs to help block out some of the background noises. Most children can wear foam earplugs comfortably. They do not block out all sounds, and the children can still hear speech at normal conversational levels when someone is talking or giving verbal instructions. The earplugs do, however, cut down on the amount of background noise the child hears, thus eliminating some of the auditory distractions.

Earplugs are also small and lightweight, so they can be easily transported to different locations. For a child who is sensitive to loud noises, it would be worthwhile to keep a pair of earplugs handy for times when loud noises interfere with the child's comfort and ability to function optimally. Plan ahead for activities like concerts and fireworks, and have the earplugs ready so everyone can enjoy the event.

My children do not wear their earplugs constantly when they do their schoolwork. They put their earplugs in when they become aware that they are being distracted by noise of any type. If I notice that they seem distracted by sounds, I will sometimes suggest use of the earplugs or ask them if the earplugs would be helpful to them. There are times when my children seem more auditorily distracted than usual. They use the earplugs as needed during these times.

<u>Tips for helping with Auditory Distractibility</u>
- *Choose a quiet work area.*
- *Minimize multiple noises when possible.*
- *Wear headphones, earmuffs or earplugs.*
- *Play classical music to mask out other sounds.*
- *Increase awareness of auditory distractions.*
- *Plan ahead for noisy situations (take earplugs along).*

I think God has allowed me to be easily distracted by noises so that I can better understand what my distractible children experience. I use a pair of earplugs myself when the atmosphere in our home seems especially noisy to me. Reducing the sounds I hear helps me concentrate on the things I need to get done, without the feeling of agitation I experience when there are multiple sources of noise occurring simultaneously. I can still have a conversation with a nearby person, but I don't hear everything that is said in another room. By wearing the earplugs myself I am also showing my children that the earplugs are useful and something to be utilized to help me, rather than some type of punishment because I am bothered by some noises.

As children get older, help them begin to recognize when they are becoming distracted or agitated by noises. Solicit their input as you experiment with the different options suggested for dealing with distracting sounds. By providing a menu of strategies to reduce or cope with auditory distractions, you will help your children develop the ability to determine and choose the options that work best for them.

Beth Boring   Age 13

Chapter 5 – Visual Distractibility

"And then the tallest guy ran into the room and there were all these fancy plates on the table and it looked like they had fried chicken on them and the guy with the dark hair grabbed the plate on the end with one hand and…" Josh retold scenes he had seen on videos with such detail that I often had difficulty discerning the main points or the plot of the story. When Josh saw a movie, he could recall minute details and remember dialogues word for word. His memory for what he'd seen amazed me because it was usually difficult for him to remember things. It took him a long time to tell me about movies he'd seen since he included such vivid and lengthy descriptions of each and every scene.

I steadfastly restricted Josh's viewing of T.V. or videos when he was young, because I wanted him to learn and experience real life as an active participant. His reaction when he was allowed to watch a video showed me that he relished the experience. Josh demonstrated such good recall even weeks after viewing a video that I suspected he was primarily a visual learner.

Because Josh was so tuned in visually, he noticed every movement within his visual range. His ability to take in information visually was an obvious strength, but it was also a weakness since this proved to be another area where Josh struggled with distractibility. His eye gaze darted around so quickly that he seemed to be afraid of missing something. It was as if he constantly scanned the environment for anything new to see, even if it was just a tiny piece of dust made visible by a stream of sunlight.

Most children are observant, often noticing things that adults are too hurried or preoccupied to see. For a child with visual distractibility, however, the tendency to see and notice everything that occurs around him is experienced to a much greater extreme. The child who swivels his head in each direction to watch whatever is happening at the moment evidences this type of distractibility. He is not able to maintain his focus and sustain eye gaze for the task at hand, but seems compelled to look at everything that moves or is visually engaging.

Josh has shown a propensity toward taking in information visually since he was a toddler. We could spend twenty minutes walking outside and only cover a short distance because of the frequent stops we made to look at interesting items Josh discovered along the way. He easily found things I would have had trouble locating if I were diligently searching for them. Yet to Josh it was perfectly natural to closely scrutinize all the things he encountered.

Josh admittedly has excellent visual skills. He remembers what he sees, and displays an amazing capacity for making detailed drawings of items he views. During schoolwork time, however, this strength is also a hindrance. Josh notices the slightest of motions, whether directly in front or him or seen out of the corner of his eye. His natural curiosity compels him to inspect more closely any source of movement, and he often leaves his work area to investigate.

Usually the source of visual distraction is not anything that requires a response from Josh. Yet he often reacts to what he has seen, wasting time playing with the cat as she walks by or going on a fly-killing mission instead of persevering with his schoolwork. He is unable to filter out irrelevant visual information and concentrate solely on what is important at the time.

Once when Josh was about five years old I sent him upstairs to clean his room. Since he spread his toys around in order to view them all at once, it did not take long for his bed and floor to be covered with toys. This did not bother Josh at all, but since the mess bothered me he headed to his room to get it cleaned up.

After about twenty minutes, I followed Josh upstairs to check on his progress. When I looked into his room, my jaw dropped with amazement and dismay. Josh had found a skein of yarn and was crouched down busily wrapping and tying yarn on objects all around his room. It looked like some kind of bizarre spider web made of yarn had trapped Josh and his toys.

When Josh noticed me standing in the doorway, he began proudly telling me about his "yarn circus". He had tied rubber bands onto one of the yarn strands and had Lego people hanging from them to perform as trapeze artists. He had even managed to weave a pair of underwear from his laundry basket into the hanging yarn strands to serve as a tent for some of the circus animals.

Not only was his room not straightened up, it was impossible to walk through without getting tripped up by the "yarn circus" with its many props. Anything Josh saw was fair game for adding to the circus, and once he got started he saw more and more activities he could set up using toys that were already on the floor of his room. He was so involved in his pursuits that he quickly forgot all about the reason he'd been sent upstairs in the first place.

Tips for helping with visual distractibility
- **_Try wearing a hat with a bill or visor_**
- **_Have a work area facing away from visual distractions_**
- **_Use a folding cardboard display board_**
- **_Use color and contrasts_**
- **_Try frames in different colors and sizes_**
- **_Use highlighters_**
- **_Try graph paper or lined paper turned sideways_**
- **_Reduce visual clutter_**

Over the years, I have tried many things to help reduce Josh's visual distractibility. Sometimes he wears a hat with a visor, which partially blocks visual distractions when he wears it low over his eyes. We have tried arranging his work area so that he is not facing a window or any other area likely to have activities or movements he would notice and watch.

One of the simplest and most effective items we have used is a folding cardboard display board. These are often used for visual displays or science fair projects, but we use ours as a study carrel. It is lightweight so it can easily be transported to use in a variety of locations. It opens up so that it can surround the student on three sides and helps block out visual distractions. It folds up fairly flat and is easily stored away until the next time it is needed. Most office supply stores carry these.

One guideline I gave Josh for using the display board as a study aid was that it needed to remain plain and undecorated. His artistic tendencies and habit of drawing on the margins of his school pages could easily have carried over to his display board, offering further distractions rather than reducing them. Stickers were also not allowed, since they gave Josh something else to look at and think about that was not related to his assigned work. I didn't think to prohibit poking holes in the cardboard, but when I discovered Josh doing that I informed him that hole poking was also unacceptable!

In order to convey to my children that we all have strategies we use to help us perform better, I occasionally model using the display board myself. My purpose is to encourage my children as they see me use the display board when I need to concentrate on my work. I want them to see it as a useful tool, acceptable to all in the family who need it. Sometimes I will wear foam earplugs while using the display board. This reassures the children that use of these tools is meant to help them and is not intended as punishment when they need to use them.

Using Color

Although Josh is colorblind, he is able to see contrasts of dark and light hues of color. This contrast helps him to focus his attention visually. Visual contrast is also helpful for children who are not colorblind. One strategy we have used to maximize the use of visual contrast is to use a brightly colored, unpatterned placemat underneath the paper being read or worked on. The placemat visually frames the child's work. Choose a placemat that is smooth and not textured so that it will not interfere with the child's written work.

For older students, a colored file folder works well. It just frames an 8 ½" x 11" piece of paper, providing an edge of color around the paper. It has a smooth surface for writing on, and loose papers can be tucked inside until they are needed. File folders are available in a wide array of colors at many office supply stores, so finding a colored file your student likes should not be difficult.

My husband and I designed what we call our *"Heads Up!"* frames to help focus attention visually. The frames consist of colored tagboard with colored, transparent cellophane filling the frames. We made them in a variety of colors varying from light yellow to darker purple and blue. The frames can be placed over written material to highlight sections of a page.

The color and contrast provided by the frames helps some children to focus their gaze for longer periods of time than they are able to without the frame. For children who are visually distractible, the frame marks their place on the page so that when they look away and then back they can easily find where they need to look.

We laminated the frames to make them more durable, and designed them in both rectangle and square patterns to fit a variety of book sizes and curriculum needs. We also tried out several different colors for the inset portion of the frame. You may need to experiment to determine which color appeals to your child the most. I preferred the darker purple color, but Josh surprised me by choosing the lightest yellow that we had as his favorite color to use.

In addition to helping maintain visual attention, the *"Heads Up!"* frames are useful for the child who feels overwhelmed when viewing an entire page of text or math problems. By placing a frame over just a portion of the page, the material seems more manageable to the child. The teacher can decide whether to use a square or rectangular frame depending on how the material is arranged on the page.

To help sustain eye gaze to a single line of print, we use the EZC Reader®. It has a blue highlighted strip along the top to aid in visual tracking along a line of text, graphs, or charts. It is 2 3/8" x 8", and is small enough to be used as a bookmark. Even proficient readers who need help maintaining concentration can benefit by the use of color to assist in focusing attention.

Similarly, the EZC Return Sweep® is a product that uses color to promote visual tracking and attention.

It has a yellow highlighted strip along the top, which is wide enough to view two lines of most texts. In addition to providing a visual reminder to continue reading to the next line, the bright yellow color encourages focused attention to the page being viewed. Its dimensions are the same as the EZC Reader®, but the highlighted strip is wider.

Visual distractibility often co-exists with incredible opportunities to learn through visual methods. The challenge for those of us who teach is to find ways to make the visual abilities serve the learner's best interests and be utilized in positive ways. It is challenging to find ways to direct the child who is easily distracted by what he sees, but it is necessary for optimal learning to occur.

Beth Boring   Age 13

Chapter 6 – Sensory Seeking and Avoiding

"Tickle my back!" begged Beckie as she grabbed my hand and guided it to her back. I could count on this request any time I sat down to read with Beckie or hold her on my lap. She just loved being tickled on her back and she craved the physical contact of cuddling. Even before she could talk, Beckie quieted as soon as I picked her up and put her cheek next to my own.

I assumed that Beckie's need for hugs and touches were due to her affectionate nature. It wasn't until we went to a craft show that I realized that Beckie's need for tactile and sensory input went far deeper than just a desire to give and receive affection.

When Beckie was three years old, I took her to a craft show with me. I knew that there would be many items at her eye level, so before we entered the room with the craft booths I instructed Beckie to "Look with your eyes, but do not touch anything." Beckie looked up at me with a combination of sadness and bewilderment as she said, "But Mommy, to touch *IS* to look." Finally, I made the connection and realized that Beckie was a strongly tactile learner. She had been giving me cues all along.

When Beckie was a baby and beginning to feed herself, she was such a messy eater that I wondered if she had difficulty chewing and swallowing. She ended up with food all over her high chair, her hands, and her face. I watched her closely, but she did not seem to be choking or having particular difficulty with any of the foods or textures we offered her. I realized much later that Beckie was deliberately crumbling and smashing her food so she could feel the different sensations provided by the experience.

When Beckie was a toddler, she delighted in pouring and digging in the sand in our sandbox. I even caught her deliberately pouring sand on her head and trickling it through her hair. Since I did not want to have to try and scrub sand off her scalp every time she played, I told her she was not allowed to pour sand on her head anymore. Beckie reluctantly complied with my command not to pour sand over her head, but a short time later I looked up to see her positioned upside down. She was grinding the top of her head back and forth in the sand, smiling happily with the discovery that she had figured out a new way to experience sand. I had to get more specific with my directions!

Sensory Avoiding
Sensory issues can be manifested in numerous ways. Some children may be extremely sensitive to tactile input. Those children with tactile defensiveness often avoid touching or being touched, since the sensation is not pleasurable to them. This may be especially true for the experience of feeling certain textures or tactile sensations. A child who is especially sensitive to tactile sensations may find certain physical experiences distracting. She may find some types of clothing to be extremely uncomfortable, although others

may see nothing obvious that would cause such discomfort. A child may need the sock seams lined up in a specific position or the tags cut out of his shirts, or else he will squirm and pick at his clothing relentlessly. Light touches seem to have an irritating effect for a child with this type of sensitivity.

One of the simplest accommodations for tactile sensitivity is to allow your child to choose clothing that feels comfortable to her. At times you may not be able to accommodate your child's preferences, but when possible allow her to wear clothing that is both acceptable to you and comfortable to her. This will eliminate a possible source of distraction for your child as well as convey that you are listening and caring about the experiences your child describes.

For example, when Josh was younger he strongly preferred loose-fitting clothing with elastic waistbands and shirts without buttons. He did not like sleeves that were fitted, and at times said that certain items of clothing bothered him although he could not always describe in what way. It just didn't feel right to him.

A child who is distracted by the sensations her own clothing causes will not be able to focus optimally on schoolwork. To imagine what the child experiences, try to recall a time when you felt something on your arm before you saw what it was. Perhaps it was a loose hair that had landed there. No doubt you were able to quickly locate the area of the sensation and remove its source so that your arm felt fine again.

If for some reason you were unable to remove the hair causing the sensation on your arm, you would probably continue to be distracted by it. It would be more difficult for you to complete tasks requiring concentration, with the ongoing irritation of feeling something on your arm that was uncomfortable. You might continue to feel annoyed by the sensation until the hair was finally removed. This, I think, is similar to some of the experiences of the child with tactile sensitivities.

Sensory issues can be truly distracting. Although he seemed to have a high tolerance for pain, Josh would wriggle constantly when I had him sit on a hard wooden chair. I originally thought that having him sit on a hard chair would help him stay alert and motivate him to complete his work in a more timely fashion. In reality, it was one more distraction as he wriggled around in his unsuccessful attempts to get comfortable. We discovered a solution to this problem: an inflatable sitting disk. It has different textures on both sides, but has enough flexibility that Josh can wiggle around a bit, without discomfort while remaining in his chair.

Sensory Seeking

Other children seem to have an unusually high need for proprioceptive and vestibular input, and appear to crave certain types of physical sensations. Proprioception is the ability to "interpret stimuli originating in muscles, joints, and other internal tissues to give information about the position of one body part in relationship to the other." Vestibular processing is the ability to "interpret stimuli from the inner ear receptors regarding head position and movement."[1]

Children who are seeking these types of sensory input often enjoy jumping, crashing into things, roughhousing, strong hugs, and other highly physical activities. Often such children seem to have a high pain tolerance, and react minimally to falls and bumps. They may seek out tasks that provide deep pressure to their muscles and joints such as pushing, pulling, or carrying heavy objects.

These children may seek out tactile input to a greater degree than most children do. My Beckie has always strongly preferred clothing made of soft or silky materials. She would often rub her cheek along the fabric of her favorite clothes. She nuzzled my shirts and stroked the sleeves when the material appealed to her, and fingered any jewelry I wore. She still does not like the way heavy material such as denim feels, but is quite comfortable in stretchy material such as spandex.

Beckie also loves going around barefoot. She would avoid shoes year-round if she could, but winters in Ohio prevent that from happening. Even when she is persuaded to wear shoes, she prefers to wear them without socks. She has conceded to wearing shoes outside in cold weather, but as soon as she's indoors the shoes come off again.

---

[1] Hopkin, H. & H. Smith (Eds.). (1993). <u>Willard and Spackman's Occupational Therapy, Eighth Edition</u>. (p.893). Philadelphia: J.B. Lippincott Company.

I used to battle constantly with Beckie as I attempted to keep socks and shoes on her feet. She didn't seem uncomfortable in them, but preferred going barefoot at every opportunity. I worried that her feet would get cold, or that she would step on something and injure her foot. When I realized that her desire to go barefoot was consistent with her need for tactile input, I stopped expecting her to wear socks and shoes at all times.

Beckie likes to experience sensations through touching, even if it is through the bottoms of her feet. She wears socks and shoes when we leave home, but around the house she is happily barefoot. When her feet feel cold, I expect Beckie to recognize that and take action to get socks or slippers on again. The first thing she does when she comes in from outside our home is to kick off her shoes. Sometimes she even remembers to put them where they belong so she can find them the next time she goes out!

I asked Beckie why she disliked wearing shoes so much, and she explained it to me. "Mom, when I wear shoes I feel like I've lost my sense of touch. When I'm barefoot, I can feel everything with the bottoms of my feet. Even if I wear my shoes without socks, all I can feel then is the inside of my shoe and that's only a rough feeling." The tactile sensations she receives through going barefoot are important to her.

When Josh was younger, he loved bumping and crashing into things with such force that I thought he would hurt himself. It never seemed to cause him anything but the mildest of discomfort, and often he did not react to the bumps and jarring at all. He seemed more surprised than hurt after finding himself on the ground again.

Beckie also engaged in activities that involved jumping and bumping, and rarely remembered how she got the bruises and scrapes on her legs that resulted from her various adventures. Often, by the time we made it to the kitchen or bathroom to wash the injured area and get a Band-Aid®, she was eager to be on her way and was unaware of any discomfort.

As Josh got older, he usually found ways to get the sensory input he needed in more acceptable and less distracting ways than when he was younger. One new development that I found unpleasant and distracting to me, however, was when Josh started cracking his knuckles. He did this throughout the day, but especially when he was feeling nervous or tense. He also stretched his arms behind his back in an attempt to ease some of his tension.

After consulting with some occupational therapists, they reminded me that knuckle-cracking provides pressure to the finger joints and they gave me some suggestions for how Josh could get that input without resorting to cracking his knuckles. I began to encourage Josh to press his hands flat against a wall and push, which provides him with input to the joints in his hands and arms. I am also happy to report that Josh has learned to do fingertip push-ups, which are much easier for me to tolerate than when I kept hearing him crack his knuckles.

Sensory Strategies

For children who are affected by sensory issues, first try to determine the types of stimulation they are seeking or avoiding.[2] For the child who seeks out strong proprioceptive or vestibular input, try incorporating pushing or lifting activities. Push-ups, jumping up and down, swinging, rocking, and pulling a wagon filled with weighted objects are excellent ways to provide sensory input. Being rolled up in a blanket or mat for a minute or two can be fun and is calming for some children.

Although Beckie usually seeks out sensory experiences, sometimes she becomes over-stimulated and tries to limit sensory input in an attempt to organize herself. Beckie likes having "hideouts" made with blankets positioned over furniture. She spreads a blanket or two over a table or chairs, and then takes some books and stuffed animals under the blanket tent with her. She stays happily in her hideout feeling secure and relaxed. She is usually less active and is quieter when she is in her hideout. Sometimes she takes a flashlight in with her and does her reading for school while she is there.

When Beckie notices something interesting, she seems compelled to see how it feels when touched and she is not intimidated by textures or appearance. Even when I took her to park programs featuring mammals or

---

[2] For further reading on sensory issues I recommend the book <u>The Out-of-Sync Child</u> by Carol Stock Kranowitz.

reptiles, Beckie eagerly touched them all when it was her turn. It made her especially happy when she was given the opportunity to hold a snake. As it slithered up her arm, she announced with a glorious smile, "It's tickling me!"

Tips for Sensory Issues

- *Be sensitive to strong clothing preferences.*
- *Incorporate activities that provide proprioceptive and vestibular input.*
- *Have a repertoire of calming activities.*
- *For sensory seekers, use manipulatives and models.*
- *For sensory avoiders, have a "hide-out" spot.*
- *Consult an occupational therapist for treatment ideas.*

Teaching Tips

I knew that when I taught Beckie she would need to feel the materials as much as possible. I chose math activities that used manipulatives, and I created my own materials when I thought of something that might work. When Beckie was learning the letters of the alphabet and their sounds, I took small pieces of wood and wrote a letter on each piece with colored glue. When the glue dried, the surface was slightly raised and Beckie could trace the letters with her fingers as we worked on each one.

I had Beckie practice writing by forming the letters with her index and middle fingers together in a baking pan filled with cornmeal, rice, or flour. In warm weather we painted letters on the sidewalk with water and an old paintbrush.

Sometimes we formed numbers or letters out of pipe cleaners or play-dough. These were not fancy or expensive methods or materials, but they appealed to Beckie because they were a good fit with her approach to learning.

Some children are better able to focus on academic tasks after they have spent some time jumping on a mini trampoline or pogo stick. Others find it relaxing to hang by their arms for several seconds on a chin-up bar or rings placed in a doorway. These activities do not have to take a great deal of time, and can be repeated as needed throughout the day.

There are also strategies that can be used while the child is working on school tasks. Try letting your child wrap up tightly in a comfortable blanket. The physical pressure of the blanket on the body has a calming, relaxing effect. Likewise, a weighted object on the lap provides the calming effect of deep pressure and serves as a tactile reminder when the child needs to remain seated.

Beckie, who consistently seeks out sensory stimulation, uses a sand-filled turtle on her lap. The turtle weighs about four pounds. It is not heavy enough to cause her legs to go to sleep or for her to experience any discomfort, but it provides constant tactile input while she works. If she forgets that she needs to remain in her seat and starts to stand up, the turtle begins to slide off her lap. This provides an immediate tactile reminder that she needs to be sitting down.

As with any strategy, present the idea in a positive fashion so that the child does not feel she is being punished or rejected. Beckie knew that she tended to move around without even realizing it, so she welcomed the sand turtle as a helper for her. She named her sand turtle "Speedy", and treated him with great care. I've seen Beckie stroking the turtle's back which provides her with another way of getting some of the tactile input she craves.

Having the turtle as a silent reminder also frees me up from the need to verbally remind Beckie to sit down. Prior to having the turtle, I found myself frequently prompting Beckie to have a seat. Sometimes she would sit down only to pop up again moments later without even thinking about it. When I would remind her to sit down again she would look surprised and stare down at her legs as if she didn't even realize she was no longer sitting in her chair!

A child who seeks out sensory input will appreciate your strong hugs and firm touches. If you notice that your child seems anxious or especially fidgety, a reassuring firm hand on the child's shoulder or back may be calming.

When Beckie was small and in seemingly constant motion, she enjoyed getting "meatball hugs". She sat on my lap, wrapped her arms around her knees, and curled up into the smallest "meatball" she could manage. I then wrapped my arms around her and gently squeezed while rocking back and forth. Beckie absolutely loved this sensation and requested "meatball hugs" often. It helped meet some of her sensory needs and had a calming effect, while at the same time reassuring her of my great affection for her.

When sensory issues are a source of continual disruption in activities of daily living, a consultation with an occupational therapist may be helpful. The therapist can complete an evaluation and make treatment suggestions to help with the various symptoms that interfere with your child's ability to function optimally.

Once I was able to identify the source of my children's seemingly quirky behaviors, then I could begin to address the needs they exposed. Listening to their explanations, asking questions to clarify, and observing their reactions to various sensory inputs are all helpful ways to determine possible accommodations. I try to have a variety of strategies for the children to use as needed, and I encourage them to think through what might be helpful to them at any given time.

Josh Boring, age 14

<u>Chapter 7 – The Fidgeter</u>

Trying to completely eliminate fidgeting may be an exercise in futility. It is better to find acceptable ways to accommodate the need for movement. Allowing small, subtle movements will ultimately be less distracting than the constant interruptions and frustrations that will occur if you respond to the many extraneous movements you observe in your child. Furthermore, your child will feel understood and accepted when you work with her to find acceptable strategies that help you both feel successful.

I remember the time I became increasingly aware that something was irritating me, filling me with the urge to twitch rhythmically as I was preparing my family's dinner. As my concentration on the recipe I was preparing weakened, I realized that the source of irritation was the sound emanating from the half door that separates the kitchen and dining rooms of my house. Josh was standing just inside the kitchen, opening and closing the door over and over and the squeaks and clicks intruded more insistently into my awareness until they were impossible to ignore. There was no ultimate goal in Josh's behavior, only a manifestation of his need to be doing something with his hands.

Josh is an accomplished fidgeter. When he was younger I tried, unsuccessfully, to eliminate his constant handling of anything within his arm's reach. Once when he was in kindergarten, I cleared his desk before beginning a lesson so he wouldn't have anything to hold or make noise with while I taught. I looked away for a moment and when I looked back he had picked up a rubber band off the floor and was stretching it this way and that. I took the rubber band away, and he was soon pulling on the drawstring of his pants. I tucked the drawstring into his pants and rolled the waistband down one roll in order to help him remember to leave the string alone. He pulled a pencil from his desk and started drumming away. I took the pencil away, and patiently asked Josh to tuck his hands under his legs just until I got done with the short lesson we needed to do. Josh readily complied, and things went smoothly for about half a minute. That's when Josh toppled sideways along with his chair, obviously pushed over by vicious air molecules!

Josh did not limit his fidgeting to certain situations. He consistently sought to have something in his hands. Even as I read aloud to my children, Josh would be doing headstands or building with Legos. I urged him to sit up and listen, but as soon as my focus moved back to the book he would be under the table or grabbing for something to handle.

Josh could pick at a hole in his pants until it was enlarged enough to fit his fist into, and then he would challenge himself by seeing how far he could fit his arm into the new entrance to his pant leg. If I caught him in time, he would try and stop his picking. But if he had nothing else in his hand soon his fingers would unconsciously stray back to the hole as if compelled to be touching and exploring something at all times.

Sometimes when the family is sitting at the table talking, Josh will be tapping his feet on the floor in a rapid cadence. The noise competes with the conversational exchange, and we have to remind Josh to stop thumping so we are not all distracted by the noise. Again, Josh does not always even realize when he is tapping away.

Beckie's fidgeting took the form of continuous movement. Even while sitting in a chair, she was continually changing positions. She rarely sat with good posture, feet flat on the floor. She shifted from side to side, sat on one foot or both feet, and squirmed. Sometimes I would catch her sitting on the arm or even the back of the chair, which was especially disruptive during mealtimes. She constantly fidgeted even while sitting on my lap, although she frequently sought out the opportunity to sit with me. Her relentless wiggling and writhing made it increasingly uncomfortable to hold her.

Beckie also needed to have something in her hands. She was not as adept as her brother was at finding small objects to handle, but she solved this by winding her fingers in my hair and fingering my earrings or necklaces. She was very gentle, but I often had to explain to others that Beckie enjoyed feeling different textures and would want to touch their hair and jewelry if they picked her up.

Selecting Fidget Items

Over the years I came to realize that my children actually seemed better able to pay attention when I allowed them to have something in their hands. If I did not allow them to handle anything, they squirmed and fidgeted so restlessly it even distracted me. So I permitted them to have small objects to hold and manipulate, but with certain boundaries in place.

Before I let my children hold an object during a teaching situation, I reviewed the rules. They were not allowed to throw the object. They could not grab another's object, or use their own to tease or annoy each other. They could not handle it in such a way that it might break. If the object were used to make noise or distract in any way, they forfeited the object for the remainder of the lesson.

I learned over time to select objects that were inherently quiet. I tended to provide the same set of items to fidget with each day, so the novelty factor wore off but the tactile sensation remained. When I first started allowing my children to use fidget toys, there was an adjustment period as they learned my expectations and explored the toys. The toys were kept in a box when they were not in use.

My daughter, Beth, does not have a need to fidget. She can sit still and attend beautifully for long periods of time. When her siblings began to use fidget toys, however, Beth felt left out. I did not want her to feel punished for her ability to sit still without having something in her hands, so I let her select a fidget toy as well and she was quite content to be included. It did not inhibit her ability to attend, and made her feel as special as her siblings who truly needed the accommodation.

As you consider items to give your children for handling, keep in mind the need to find something quiet so it does not present further distractions. Also choose something relatively small so that it can be held in one hand and can be easily transported from location to location.

I give my children choices in selecting what they handle. I have a number of items that are quiet and small, and I encourage the children to pick an item that is appealing to them. They do not pick the same item each time, and they like having the variety to choose from. Since I compiled the objects, I know they are all quiet and portable and I am satisfied with any choice they make.

Some Of My Favorite Fidget Items

Wikki Stix® are wax-covered strings and one of my favorite fidget toys. They come in a variety of lengths and colors. The strings are reusable and can be cut but will not break. The children can form various shapes with them, and they can be used to form diagrams or models as part of school work. They can be put on dry erase boards and are easily removed. A dab of lemon juice removes any wax residue. Best of all, they can be wrapped and unwrapped around fingers or pencils while making no noise and meeting the need of children who seek out objects to manipulate with their hands.

I also use helium strength balloons filled with flour or rice. When I make them, I strive to fill the balloon until it is the right size to comfortably fill the palm of one hand. I have special rules for the fidget balloons, and I check the balloons regularly for signs of wear. Because they are just balloons, they will break eventually and flour or rice could make quite a mess.

To extend the use of the balloon, I have a rule that the balloon can only be held in one hand at a time. The child can switch the balloon from hand to hand as desired. The "one hand at a time" rule makes it very difficult for the child to twist and pull on the balloon in such a way that it could burst. I also have the rule that the child is not allowed to poke the balloon with a pencil or other object, and is not allowed to try and push her finger through to the other side.

Koosh balls® or other textured balls make nice fidget toys for a child who can discipline himself not to throw or bounce it. The balls feel differently in the hand depending on whether the child holds it gently or firmly. Some types of balls have an elastic quality that allows them to be stretched or squished before they return to their original shape. Textured balls or pieces of clay provide yet another tactile sensation when rolled under the palm of the hand on a flat surface such as a desktop.

One of Beckie's favorite fidget items is a sealed plastic bag with hair gel and small toys or erasers inside. She can squish the hair gel around and explore the feel of the different objects with her fingertips. Sometimes she even sniffs at the bag to get a whiff of the hair gel scent. I always use two bags with the seals at opposite sides and clear packaging tape to reinforce the seal for this fidget item, because exuberant squeezing could cause the gel to squirt out if the bag leaks.

Another good fidget item is a polished stone, which can be rubbed or rolled around in the hand. I know a few adults who have a smooth sphere on their key chains that they like to finger. Just as some adults jingle their keys or coins in their pockets, some children may learn to cope with their need to fidget by finding objects they can use to help themselves focus and feel calmer. As children get older and learn to recognize for themselves strategies that prove helpful, they may benefit from a few carefully selected objects to keep in their pockets or in another easily accessible location.

Melinda's Rules for Fidget Toys
- *No throwing or bouncing the fidget toy.*
- *Keep it quiet.*
- *Handle it properly.*
- *Choose something small.*
- *Have a variety of objects to choose from.*
- *Do not stretch, bend, poke, punch, twist or otherwise handle the toy in such a way that it will break.*

For those times when the fidgeting seems to extend to full body movements, sitting on a large therapy ball might be helpful. Select a ball that is appropriate for the child's size. The child needs to be sitting so that his feet are flat on the floor and with his knees bent at a right angle so his hips stay in good alignment. This will allow the child to gently bounce on the therapy ball while staying in one place. Once the need for movement is met, the child is free to concentrate on other activities and may be better able to attend to academic work.

Beckie sits at a desk for some of her work. On days when she especially needs to move around, she sits on the ball and continues working at her desk. I've noticed that even her handwriting improves when she sits with her feet flat on the floor, and sitting on the therapy ball promotes that kind of good posture. She can wiggle around from side to side and bounce gently up and down when she wants to, but is able to continue working on the task at hand. When she wiggles without the ball, she is often sitting on her foot or positioned at an angle that makes pencil and paper tasks more difficult to complete.

Beckie is on the ball!

Josh uses a larger therapy ball than Beckie does, and uses it for brief periods of time when he is working at our coffee table. Besides using the ball to sit on, Josh sometimes lies over the ball on his stomach. He places the book he's reading on the floor, and gently rolls on the ball while he reads. He is comfortable in that position, and by allowing himself to move as he needs to, he is more relaxed and able to concentrate better on his reading material.

Some children wiggle constantly in their seats. They rock the chair from side to side or back and forth, putting excessive stress on the chair legs and even tipping themselves and the chair over at times. There does not seem to be a chair in existence that is comfortable enough for these children to settle down and cease their constant motion.

When Josh was in the first grade we sat on the couch together for our reading times, so that Josh could be on one side of me and Beth could be on the other side as we shared books. Our couch was comfortable. In fact, I often found myself becoming drowsy as the children read aloud. Yet it was not uncommon for me to turn toward Josh and find not his head but his rear end beside me as he put his head on the floor! Now if you think teaching a child to read can be challenging, try teaching someone who cannot sustain eye gaze to a printed word or keep their head within the vicinity of the book. I felt beyond challenged.

For children like this, try an inflatable sitting disk. This gives the same sort of input to the body as sitting on a therapy ball, but the disk takes up less room and is more portable. This is especially nicer for older students, as it is less conspicuous than the therapy ball. The commercially available cushion disks have appealed to Josh as much as the therapy balls did when he was younger. The sitting disk allows him to remain seated while making gentle, controlled movements from side to side or up and down. Before he sits down, Josh always looks around to locate the cushion disk so he can position it on whatever chair he chooses. He finds it quite comfortable.

Josh concentrates comfortably!

Some disks allow the user to adjust the degree of inflation to individualize the desired degree of cushion firmness. These disks have the advantage of being portable and taking up little space for storage. As with the therapy balls, rules for using the cushion disk must be clearly explained before the child is given one to use.

Although the disks are built with sturdy materials, they are not designed to be used as Frisbees® or rolled down hallways!

Some people use a partially inflated beach ball to allow for limited movements while sitting on a chair. Although a beach ball is less sturdy than the commercially available sitting disks, it may be a good way to experiment and see if the child responds well to using it. The child may continue wiggling, but possibly to a lesser degree and without rocking the entire chair. Set the rules before providing the disk or beach ball so the child will know not to poke the ball with a pencil or engage in any other activity that might damage the ball or disk.

It helps to remember that even though a child may be fidgeting, she may still be hearing and understanding what you are saying. I used to be very frustrated by Josh's moving around when I was reading to him. He was all over the place – under the table, standing on his head, hanging over the side of the couch, or just doing what appeared to me as random motions. Josh's father and I frequently exhorted him to "Sit up and listen." Josh claimed that he was listening, but we didn't understand how he could possibly incorporate what he heard while he was being so physically active.

One day in frustration, Josh's Dad gave him the usual exhortation to sit up and listen and Josh gave his usual reply that he was listening. His Dad asked Josh to prove that he had been listening by retelling the story we'd been reading. From under the table, Josh gave a surprisingly accurate account of the story. Furthermore, he correctly answered comprehension questions about the story and offered some of his own opinions about the story itself. We were amazed and humbled. We apologized to Josh for not believing him when he told us he was listening.

Josh still had to learn to sit quietly and listen in a more conventional manner at times, but we became much more accepting of his need to move around while he listened. In fact, we realized that it took so much self-restraint and concentration for Josh to sit still that there was little energy left to focus on what was said. He actually was able to learn more effectively when allowed to move around when he felt the need.

Recognizing and accepting a child's need to fidget will eliminate unnecessary battles between child and adult. The child who fidgets may not understand why he fidgets and may not even be aware of his own fidgeting behavior. He may have no idea how to cope with it in acceptable ways. With compassion and creativity, adults and children can work together to develop strategies that work.

Josh Boring, age 14

Chapter 8 – The Hyperactive

There are times when children just need a small amount of movement, and are merely fidgety. At other times, the need to move around involves the entire body in gross motor activities that use the child's large muscle groups. These are the children who are recognized as having such excess energy they are sometimes called hyperactive.

Some children just seem to have so much energy that they can't contain it and it spills out through their actions. Josh and Beckie both have a high energy level. When they were very young, it was exhausting to watch them and keep them safe because I had to be on constant vigil as they relentlessly explored every environment they encountered. Unfortunately for me, I was not similarly blessed with their degree of energy and it was difficult for me during their early years when my sleep was often interrupted or shortened. They did not nap as long as most children their ages, and did not remain in one location for more than a minute or two for most of their waking hours.

When Josh was a preschooler, he would wake up early in the morning and burst into my room announcing "Mom! It's another day!" I appreciated his enthusiasm, even as I admittedly struggled to share it on some mornings, especially before my first cup of coffee. Josh woke up ready to face the day with full energy from the time he opened his eyes in the morning until he reluctantly fell asleep at night. I learned to drink coffee at room temperature, because chasing Josh kept me so busy that my coffee had usually cooled off before I had the chance to drink it.

The only times Josh slowed down during the day were times when he was sick and running a fever. If he ever fell asleep during the day, I knew he was ill. He rarely reduced speed if he felt just mildly unwell, and has always had a high tolerance for the pain associated with illness and minor injuries. His usual pace was fast, faster, fastest!

Josh's hyperactivity had some unexpected effects on me. At times I found myself unable to complete coherent thoughts because I could not focus on Josh's actions and concentrate on what I wanted to say at the same time. Occasionally, as I attempted to teach Josh, he would be jumping around and I'd suddenly realize that my head was bobbing up and down as I tried to maintain eye contact. Sometimes Josh would come to me and begin telling me about an event he had observed outside, but my concentration on his words lapsed as he bumped into furniture and flung himself upside down over the sofa while he spoke.

A high activity level can interfere with schoolwork in a number of ways. It can make handwriting less legible as the child shifts her posture repeatedly while writing. Tables and desks get bumped, affecting not only the active child but also anyone else who is sharing the workspace. High- energy actions can distract the teacher, other students, and the child herself.

Redirecting or Releasing Energy

I have found two general approaches to working with my hyperactive children, and tend to alternate between them as I see what works on a given day. The approaches can be categorized as those that attempt to <u>direct or subdue</u> actions, and those that attempt to provide a <u>release or outlet</u> for the bursts of high energy that occur.

To promote a calming effect, try firmly placing your hand on the child's shoulder or back, letting your hand rest in one spot for several seconds. Experiment with the various ideas presented in chapter six that dealt with sensory issues. Make sure the child is physically comfortable wherever she is seated. Try to reduce any extraneous sights, sounds, and smells that might contribute to the child's physical agitation.

When you discern that the child needs to move and has excess physical energy, try to find acceptable ways for that energy to be expended. I keep a number of items for safe physical activities that allow the child to be active even indoors during inclement weather. A five minute break spent on physical activity can help some children return to less active tasks with greater alertness and relaxation.

A child who is hyperactive will find things to do on his own. Since many hyperactive individuals also tend to be impulsive, the physical activities chosen may be dangerous. I have tried to set boundaries in place to keep my children safe from behaviors that put them at risk for injury. Yet my children have done a few things I never thought to specifically mention to them, so the boundaries have needed adjustments and clarification over time.

I'll never forget the time my daughters came rushing into my bedroom all out of breath. "Mom! Mom! Josh is on the garage roof!" It is a testament to my previous experiences with Josh that I didn't waste a moment questioning or disbelieving the girls. I rushed to the window that faced our garage, and saw Josh casually making his way across the roof. Being careful to keep my voice calm so as not to startle him, I called out to him and asked what he was doing up on the roof.

He looked at me and seemed genuinely surprised to see me, but then calmly explained that he had thrown the dog's Frisbee® and it landed on the roof. So he found a way to climb up to get it. Clearly, to Josh, this was the logical course of action. I told him to carefully get down off the roof and he informed me that he had been on his way to do just that when I started talking to him.

Fortunately, Josh's martial arts training has helped him develop good balance and coordination, and he was able to get back down off the roof without incident. To Josh's surprise and disappointment, I had to add "no getting up on the garage roof" to the list of prohibitions designed to keep him safe. For now, climbing a tree will have to suffice when he wants a higher perspective for viewing the world. (I'll get the dog a new Frisbee® if I have to!)

Quick Exercises for Energy Output

- *Stationary bike riding.*
- *Mini-trampoline jumping.*
- *Jump on Pogo sticks, pogo-balls, or jump ropes.*
- *Stretching (especially arms and legs).*
- *Marching.*

One of Josh's favorite energy outlets has been riding on a stationary bike. He experiments with his speed and the force he exerts, and sometimes keeps the pace steady while completing some of his reading. Our bike has a timer, so Josh can set it for a pre-determined amount of time and the ringing bell of the timer reminds him when it's time to get back to another task. Exercise and physical conditioning are added benefits.

Another item that we've used both indoors and outside is a mini-trampoline. It is a nice way for a child to bounce within a defined area while developing balance and coordination in addition to expending excess energy. Our favorite way to use the mini-trampoline is to put on some upbeat music and jump for the duration of a song or two.

Pogo sticks or pogo balls can be excellent outlets for a quick release of energy. Some pogo toys come with sound effects to encourage the child to continue jumping to the beat. Others are equipped with counters to help the child keep track of the highest number of continuous jumps they have attained. Children develop physical conditioning and improve their motor coordination while jumping away spare energy.

Jumping rope is an excellent way to improve stamina, develop coordination, and release pent-up energy. Beckie just loves using a jump rope that plays music and other interesting sound effects. All of my kids have used the Band Buddies Jump Rope®, which they assembled themselves from a kit. The kit includes brightly colored rubber bands and the necessary instructions and hardware for the completion of one jump rope. The resulting product is their own bright, stretchy jump rope that they helped to make.

Many of my ideas for releasing energy involve jumping activities because those involve the entire body, increase the heart and respiration rate, and provide a level of physical stimulation and input to the joints that children typically seek out and enjoy. I will gladly provide my children with opportunities for jumping that are acceptable to me and give them options that do not involve jumping on the furniture!

Another way to release excess energy and physical tension is through stretching. Controlled stretching of major muscle groups can be relaxing and invigorating. This is an activity that the teacher can do along with the children and enjoy the same benefits they do. It does not involve a great deal of time, and can be done without equipment or in an area with limited space in which to move about.

Moving While Learning

There are times when my children are giving indications that they need to be in motion, and I am reluctant to stop the educational flow for another break. I have a number of activities that allow for movement to be incorporated while still working on an academic task. This accommodates my goal of accomplishing a set amount of work while also accommodating their need to move around.

I encourage my children to work on their spelling words by taking one marching step for each letter in the word. They can stand at their desks, look at the words, and say each letter out loud as they march. Another option is to allow the children to devise their own movements to accompany the letters in the spelling words.

I also encourage my children to trace spelling words with their fingers either in the air or on their desks. They say each letter out loud as they write it, and say the entire word when it is complete. I am engaging as many of their senses as possible, which will help them to retain the information since they are active in the learning process.

I suggest marching as an aid to memorization, but if one of the children wants to try a squat maneuver or some other movement for each item they are memorizing, I encourage that as well. Since one of my goals is to have my children independently determine the ways they learn most effectively, I often let them try their ideas and later help them evaluate the results and effectiveness of their strategies.

Beckie uses a video series (U Can Do®) to practice her math facts. She has separate tapes for addition, subtraction, multiplication, and division. Each tape is designed to be multi-sensory in its presentation to accommodate all learning styles. For each math fact group, the video shows a small group of children reciting the facts as they sing a song. Each song incorporates different movements, and the math facts are displayed along the top of the screen. This is excellent for visual, auditory, and tactile-kinesthetic learners as all of the senses become involved when the child exercises and recites along with the children on the videotape.

The appeal of these videos for Beckie is the musical aspect. She has always been very responsive to music, and the tunes help her to remember the math facts. By having the visual display and the motions along with the songs, she is a fully active participant in learning and memorization. The exercises are an outlet for her need to move around and allow her to get some work done while meeting that need. Later, she completes the written timed drills that are included in the booklets that come with the tape.

Marching is another exercise that does not require equipment or much space. The child can march in place for a set amount of time, during a song, or while counting up to a designated number. My children were taught to march using arms and legs together to get greater body involvement. As the child marches, he could touch his upraised left knee with his right hand, then touch the right knee with his left hand. This is known as cross - marching, and is believed to be beneficial since the movements, which cross the midline of the body, involve the use of both hemispheres of the brain.[3]

The benefit associated with performing movements which cross the body's midline is one reason why martial arts is an activity frequently recommended for children who are hyperactive, impulsive, or have difficulty sustaining attention. There are a number of different styles of martial arts, and the teaching content and approach varies from school to school. It is important to interview any instructor prior to beginning any classes to ascertain that the instructor's philosophy and teaching methods are consistent with the values and skills you want your child to learn.

Benefits of Sports

Josh and Beth both started their martial arts training at the same time. Josh was eight years old and Beth was seven, and I had interviewed the instructor over the phone and in person prior to their first class. I also asked for a "trial class" so that I could observe and ask any further questions before I committed to signing them up for classes. Once my questions had been answered satisfactorily and I felt like a working relationship had been initiated with the instructor, I signed Josh and Beth

---

[3] Dennison, Paul E. & Gail E. Dennison, (1994). <u>Brain Gym, Teacher's Edition Revised,</u> (p.4). California: Edu-Kinesthetics, Inc.

up for classes. A few years later Beckie began taking classes, too.

Martial arts as a sport is especially beneficial for children who have difficulty participating in team sports. It allows the children to work at their own paces and it has built-in individual goals as the children prepare to advance to the next belt level. The child gains experience with group instruction and learns to develop the skills needed for competition and good sportsmanship. Much of the work can be practiced alone or one-on-one, thus alleviating some of the stress factors that can occur in larger group activities. Since martial arts can be practiced all year round, there is continuity and stability over time.

The physical benefits of martial arts include increased muscle strength and flexibility and improved balance. As with other forms of exercise, the study of martial arts promotes an acceptable way for energy to be expended. Tension and stress are relieved and the child develops improved physical coordination. This also contributes to improved self-control and confidence.

Swimming offers similar benefits since it can be done all year round, involves the entire body, and can be done individually or in a group. My children have enjoyed learning to swim and then participating competitively as part of a swim team. I have seen their physical endurance improve in addition to developing greater muscle tone and coordination. They swim for enjoyment as well as the physical benefits to their health.

Beckie, my exceptionally sensory-seeking child, loves the sensations that result as she moves in various ways through the water. She has invented more than a few of her own strokes and underwater maneuvers, but seems able to remember the standard forms when she is in a swim meet. I have noticed that after Beckie has been swimming, she is better able to sit quietly in one place and seems less physically restless. Her appetite also increases after she has been swimming.

There are many options for incorporating physical activities into daily routines, either to coincide with curricular objectives or as separate activities. For children who are hyperactive, there is no adequate substitute for physical movement and exercise. Finding enjoyable outlets for energy will be worth the effort in benefits to the child and the family, and may help eliminate some of the undesirable ways hyperactivity can manifest when there is no outlet readily available.

Josh Boring, age 14

<u>Chapter 9 – The Daydreamer</u>

Even as a preschooler, Josh stared off into space and appeared to be lost in thought. When I asked him what he had been thinking about he was generally unable to tell me. I was so concerned that I asked our pediatrician if he thought Josh was possibly having seizures, but the doctor was sure that wasn't the case.

When we worked at our dining room table, I noticed Josh staring out the window. When I pulled the curtains so he wouldn't be distracted by outside activity, Josh stared at the curtains. I decided if I could determine what he was thinking about I might be able to figure out a way to lessen the amount of time he spent "in his own little world".

I started asking him questions about what he was looking at, or how he was feeling when he was staring off. He told me that when he got bored he had his own little world where he imagined various activities taking place. I had Josh describe them to me and asked him questions to clarify what he said so I could comprehend his experiences. His enthusiasm for sharing seemed to grow as he realized I was truly interested in understanding his thoughts and feelings.

I did not want to discourage Josh's creativity, which I perceived to be one of his greatest strengths. Still, I could not let it continually interfere with his completion of academic tasks, either. So we reached a compromise. When I saw that Josh was staring off again,

I would remind him to think about those things later and concentrate on his school work first. When it was time for a break, he could tell me all about what was happening in "his own little world".

Josh daydreamed so much of the time that the entire family learned about his ideas. Once when Josh had been teasing and annoying his little sister, Beckie, she suggested "Why don't you just go back to your own little world?!" Fortunately, Josh has a good sense of humor and found his sister's remark to be hilariously funny.

As Josh got older, he spent less time daydreaming. One day I was complimenting him on his improved ability to limit daydreaming. He grinned and looked at me, then asked, "Mom, do you know why I stopped going to my own little world?" I was hoping to hear him say that my love and patience had helped him, but instead he told me, "It's because you kept showing up there!" It was true. I had asked questions and listened to Josh's descriptions so many times that I became a part of Josh's "own little world".

I have tried a number of strategies to cut down on the amount of daydreaming during school time. Sometimes a tri-fold cardboard display board helps since it limits what is seen other than school work. I keep the board free of any stickers or doodling to eliminate visual distractions. It folds flat for easy storage and can be moved to new locations or work areas as needed.

I have also used headphones and a cassette tape with occasional chirping noises on it. The periodic noises serve as auditory cues, helping Josh to "stay on target." I recorded chirping sounds made by a little toy bird at random intervals on a cassette tape. I instructed Josh to listen to the tape, and when he heard the chirping sound it should remind him to check to see if he was on task with what he needed to be working on at the time. I often used a written list of tasks along with the auditory prompting of the cassette tape so Josh could visually refer to them and reorient himself back to the task of the moment.

The chirping tape served a dual purpose, because it helped Josh to self-monitor his attention, and it spared me from having to constantly redirect or verbally prompt Josh to get back to work. By listening to the tape with headphones, Josh got the prompting he needed and it did not disturb anyone else. Additionally, the bird chirping on the tape was an impersonal reminder with no frustration or fatigue expressed, unlike my own sometimes weary reminders.

Do You Sense Time Passing?

When Josh is in a daydreaming mode, he does not have an accurate sense of time passing by. To help him realize that he is spending his time nonproductively, I place a timer in front of him. Sometimes I just use my kitchen timer with its audible ticking to prompt Josh. This may help Josh focus, or the ticking may serve as another distraction, depending on the day.

One of my favorite and most frequently used tools is a timer with a red visual display. I can set it for up to sixty minutes at a time, and the red display disappears from the clock-face as time elapses. This gives the child a visual image of time passing, and is helpful in developing a better internal sense of the passage of time. It offers an additional advantage over other timers in that it is entirely silent and therefore produces no auditory distractions.

I used such a timer with Beckie before she was able to tell time on her own. It helped her to recognize how long she needed to practice the piano or spend reading. It has also been useful when we needed to go somewhere, because I could set the timer and Beckie could tell at a glance how much longer we had until our departure time.

Even though Josh could tell time, he didn't have a good internal sense of time passing. When he was engaged in a highly interesting activity, time seemed to speed by. Likewise, a low interest activity felt like hours to him when in reality only minutes had passed. The timer with the visual display helped him see for himself the passage of time. It was also an objective source difficult for Josh to argue with, unlike his responses when others tried to persuade him regarding the passage of time.

The timer I use, the Time Timer®, is an 8" square size. It runs on one AA battery and is very lightweight. It has a base for standing on a flat surface, or it can hang on the wall if desired. These features make it easy to transport the timer to any location I choose. I can set it on top of the piano or the computer monitor, to serve as a reminder of the time allotted for certain activities. It is large enough to be seen from across the room, so I can easily monitor it as the children use it.

When Josh slips into his daydreaming mode, I set the timer for about 30 minutes and place it directly in front of him as a reminder that he is wasting time. As I put the timer directly into his line of vision, I calmly tell Josh that I notice he is not using his time well and that I want to help him recognize when this is occurring. I advise Josh that he can improve in his time management skills but he will need to work on developing in that area.

At that point, I find it best if I walk away and let the timer serve as a reminder that time is passing rather than offering repeated verbal prompts and reprimands. If Josh continues to choose daydreaming over working or resets the timer himself without my permission, then there needs to be a consequence for him. Spending all of my time with an unmotivated child who is wasting time feels more like a consequence for me.

When a child does not have a good internal sense regarding the passage of time, it may be helpful to have her predict how long she thinks a given task will take. This can help the child begin to develop a realistic idea of how long her work will take her to complete, as the actual time needed is compared to the predicted amount of time. When a timer is nearby, it can also serve as a reminder to concentrate on the work at hand.

Sometimes a child is overwhelmed before even beginning a lesson if she thinks that an assignment will take a very long time. Beckie used to think that her math would take her a long time to complete, so I asked her to predict how long she thought it would take to get it finished. She sadly told me "Two hours!" I set a timer with a visual display for one hour, and told her we would reset it if necessary when the hour was over. Thirty minutes later, she finished her math work and was genuinely surprised to see time remaining on the timer's display. She saw what she was capable of doing when she disciplined herself to work rather than complaining or trying to avoid difficult tasks.

Consequences for Dawdling

Every family has ways of determining appropriate consequences for a child's actions, and it is not my intention to address the topic of disciplinary instruction within the scope of this book. I will share some thoughts, however, which may stimulate your thinking regarding the issue of daydreaming and wasting time.

I like to complete tasks, including schoolwork, in a timely manner. There are times, however, when my children are far less motivated than I am to finish their work. I used to persist in working toward the goal of completing our lessons no matter how long it took. Sometimes it took a very long time, and nothing else got done around the house. Josh can easily stretch a twenty-minute assignment over two hours.

When my children genuinely don't understand a concept, I am willing to spend more time on it until they do. I get very frustrated, however, when the issue is not one of understanding but rather of compliance or motivation. If they know what they need to get done, but are goofing off and wasting their time and mine, it is an issue of compliance and not a lack of comprehension.

I work very hard to plan lessons and teach my children in ways that will engage their interest. I cannot maintain a high level of concentration around the clock, though, and I cannot always be entertaining or highly enthusiastic each minute of the day. I am not one who naturally operates with high energy and exuberance, but I do attempt to make home schooling both effective and enjoyable for the family.

In reality, much of our daily routines consist of mundane tasks that few would consider to be great fun. When my children complain of being bored, I remind them that there will always be things needing done which are not fun but are necessary tasks. I give them examples of chores their father and I do, not because we gain enjoyment from them but because it is the responsible thing to do. There is much more to life than entertainment and pleasure, and it is a disservice to children to teach them otherwise.

Rather than looking at daydreaming as a by-product of boredom, I view it as an opportunity to practice self-discipline. Keeping daydreams under control is simply good and valuable training for reality; in fact, some measure of it is necessary just to survive day-to-day life!

I tell my children since many activities of daily living are routine, it is good that they are learning to deal with their boredom at a young age. They will have many opportunities to practice self-discipline as they overcome their aversion to tasks they perceive to be dull. I no longer offer lists of suggestions to solve their boredom issues, but allow them to fully experience these aspects of life that we all must learn to respond properly to over time.

To Minimize Daydreaming:
- *Allow time for sharing and developing ideas.*
- *Try a tri-fold cardboard display.*
- *Use headphones and a "reminder" cassette.*
- *Use a timer to remind about passing time.*
- *Let the <u>student</u> experience consequences.*
- *Teach appropriate responses to boredom.*

Sometimes my children seem unable to settle down to the task presented to them. I talk to them about the need to get their work done in a timely manner. If that seems to have no effect, I put a time limit on how long I will spend working with them on that particular subject. I share this time limit with my children so that they are fully aware of how long they have to complete their work. The amount of time I allow is reasonable, and allows for a small margin of extra time for unexpected interruptions or additional help.

If they do not finish the work within the allotted time frame, they forfeit their "free" time in the evening and have to complete their "homework" with their Dad (the "Principal") when he gets home. I stop at the predetermined time, showing them that I take my use of time seriously and will be consistent to follow through with the time limitations I have stated. The children don't like having to admit to their father that they have work to do because they wasted time during the day and didn't get it done.

This has been a beneficial strategy for our family, and one that has prevented increased stress and burnout for me, the primary teacher. I know my limits, and it is impossible for me to remain in a good teaching mode for marathon sessions. Assigning unfinished work as homework gives me a break from teaching, and allows Scott greater involvement in the children's schoolwork.

When Scott participates in homework with the kids, he comes in with a fresher approach because he hasn't been teaching and working with them all day. It's an easy task for him to do because he doesn't have to plan the assignment or teach the material. He just helps them get the work done in a supervisory capacity. The end result is that the work gets completed, the children experience the consequences for their own choices, and their Dad has a better idea of the children's understanding and approach to their schoolwork.

Even in homes with only one parent doing all the schooling, this idea can be adapted based on the developmental level of the child involved. If the child understands the work needing to be done, other activities can be eliminated or postponed until the assignment is completed. During the time allotted for the child to be working, the parent continues her own usual activities until the child indicates that the work has been finished.

The parent can check the work and remind the child that completing work in a timely manner actually affords more time for other activities.

Beth Boring age 13

Chapter 10 – Social Communication Skills

I wouldn't say that Josh completely lacked social skills as a youngster. It was more a matter of his responding to people in ways that were neither predictable nor conventionally accepted. Josh genuinely liked people and showed great interest in their activities. But certain social skills that came naturally as part of development in most children eluded him.

I had to observe and analyze Josh while he interacted with others in order to determine what he did that set him apart in negative ways. This was painful to do at times, but not as painful as doing nothing to help him and watching him fail relationally without knowing why. I needed to think through each component of communication in order to ascertain which ones Josh was omitting or overusing. It made me look at communication in a completely different light.

Josh related to others in such a way that he was frequently misunderstood and frustrated. In order to help him, I felt like I needed to be a detective and determine what skills were missing that kept Josh from being an effective communicator. At the same time, I didn't want Josh to feel like I was rejecting him or scrutinizing his every move in order to continually correct him.

Trying to teach social communication skills to any child is a sensitive issue because it addresses personal styles of relating. I approached Josh with the notion that I had observed his frustration when he had difficulty communicating and I had some ideas we could try that might help. This approach was unthreatening and accepting, because Josh knew I understood his struggles and wanted to help him succeed. I had to get beyond the idea that Josh just had odd ways of relating to others, and figure out exactly what he did that was unusual.

Eye Contact

One of the first things I noticed was that Josh did not make consistent eye contact with others. He would glance fleetingly at a person's eyes, but then would be looking all around while he talked or listened to the other person. By now I realized that Josh could hear and comprehend spoken words without needing to look at the speaker. There is a social component to eye contact during communication, however, that could not be accomplished in any other way but by looking at the other person.

I sensed that sometimes Josh was so overcome with extraneous stimulation that maintaining eye contact proved too intense an experience for him. I verbally prompted him to look at me when we talked, and he tried to comply. Still, his eye contact was limited to a brief glance, even when I held his face in my hands so that he was facing directly toward me.

The next thing I tried was the goal of having Josh make eye contact while we counted to three together. Even this was a challenge at first. I worked to make my facial expression neutral and relaxed, so it would not be too intense for Josh as he absorbed all the details. As he developed his ability to sustain eye gaze, I gradually increased the amount of time and added in new components such as watching my eyes while I talked to him and when he talked to me.

Eventually, Josh started making eye contact more frequently on his own, although I still prompted him at times. Because I knew Josh was attracted to novelty, there were times when I would silently make a funny face to reward him for looking at me when he talked. This amused him and motivated him to keep an eye on me to see what I might do next! I am not necessarily recommending this as a method of teaching eye contact, but I am suggesting that you exercise creativity in making communication enjoyable for your child.

Josh was also motivated to work on the skill of making eye contact when I explained to him that if you don't look at people they can't tell if you are listening to what they say and they might think you are not interested in them. I pointed out to him the importance of nonverbal cues such as body posture and facial expression. These are aspects of communication that you miss if you are not looking at the person as you interact with them.

Because Josh truly cared about people, he was motivated to learn ways to show it. We did a lot of role-playing together, both of desirable and undesirable methods of communicating so that the contrast would be very obvious. Once Josh understood that people feel more connected and cared for when eye contact occurs, he made a greater effort to include that in his communication repertoire. With practice, making eye contact begins to feel less uncomfortable and gradually begins to generalize to everyday exchanges.

I often prompted Josh to look at me when I needed to give him directions or discipline him for a wrongdoing. Over time, I realized that most of the times I was requesting eye contact were times when my facial expression probably wasn't the most pleasant. One day, as an experiment I made myself "freeze" my expression prior to telling Josh to look at me. Then I looked at myself in the mirror, and realized that most of the time when Josh was told to look at me he was getting to see my face with a serious or even angry expression on it.

After seeing my facial expression in the mirror, I thought it was no wonder Josh was reluctant to make eye contact! From that point on I made a concerted effort to have Josh look at me for positive comments as well, and tried to tone down the negative expressions. Sometimes I would ask Josh to look at me and when he complied I would tell him I loved him and was proud of the way he shared with his sisters or demonstrated self-control even though he was upset. I wanted him to see positive expressions as often as possible, so he would find it rewarding to look at and interact with others.

Staying on Topic

Another huge deficit in Josh's social communication skills was in the realm of making appropriate responses. There were times when Josh's creative mind was operating at such a rapid rate that he would make a remark that seemingly had nothing to do with the topic of discussion. He had so many ideas, often simultaneously vying for his attention, that he seemed to have difficulty expressing them in an understandable sequence. He was often the only one who knew what comment in the conversation had stimulated his thinking on a given topic.

When Josh said something that was irrelevant to the topic of conversation, I redirected him to the subject being discussed. I did this simply by stating "We are talking about _____ right now." Sometimes that was adequate to get Josh back to the subject. Other times, though, Josh was so absorbed with his ideas that he wanted to change the subject entirely. It helped him when I let him know we would talk about his ideas later, but first we would finish the topic that had already been initiated.

It was not an unusual occurrence at our house to have Josh pick out one word in a conversation and start thinking about that word in an entirely new context. While the rest of us continued our original conversation, Josh's thoughts would be leading him in an entirely different direction.

Sometimes it felt as though Josh took a topic, gave it a dizzying spin, and we only realized he was not thinking about what the rest of us were when his comments orbited our way as if on a collision course. Josh would say something so far removed from what the rest of us were talking about that at times we were momentarily silenced in bewilderment. Josh, seeing our puzzled expressions, was happy to backtrack and explain how he had arrived at his ideas.

Responding to Others

Another social skill I had to teach Josh was that he needed to respond outwardly in some fashion when someone talked to him or asked him a question. I was intimately familiar with Josh's patterns of relating, but even I couldn't always tell if Josh had heard me and was thinking about what I said or if he hadn't heard me at all. His facial expression often didn't alter as he processed what he heard. He generally continued in whatever activity he had been doing at the time a conversation was initiated, not even pausing to give any sign that he was aware of another's presence.

To further complicate matters, Josh took a little more time than most people to process what he heard. When he talked with people, they often expected an immediate, verbal response from him. This is how most people converse back and forth, and the pace is usually pretty rapid. When Josh hesitated in forming his response, the speaker addressing him would often repeat the question or quickly move on to talk with someone else. The assumption was that Josh did not understand or intend to answer, since his response was not as immediate as expected. I taught Josh a few strategies to use to prevent additional difficulties in this type of situation.

I explained to Josh that when he didn't answer right away people could not tell if he was listening or paying attention to them. This was especially true if he was not making eye contact with the speaker at the time. I encouraged Josh to work on this skill by telling him I knew he had a lot of ideas and thoughts to share, and I wanted to help him convey his thoughts to others. Josh truly had no idea where to start to make changes, since he could not make himself process any faster.

I offered some suggestions to get him started. The first point I taught was that there needs to be some kind of immediate response when a person has spoken to you. It does not always need to be a verbal response. Since Josh was not always able to verbalize his response instantaneously, I taught him to hold up one finger and say something he had memorized like "Let's see here" or "I need to think for a minute" to let the other person know of his intent to respond. (His favorite phrase has become "Hold on a minute.") Using this strategy reduced the number of missed opportunities and misunderstandings for Josh, and provided him with some needed additional time to formulate his responses.

There were also times when a speaker used a rapid rate of speech or used words that Josh was not familiar with and he genuinely did not know how to respond to what was said. For this type of situation, I taught Josh to ask the speaker to repeat what was said. If the meaning remained unclear to Josh, he learned to say, "I'm not sure what you mean. Could you say it in a different way?" Most people are willing to accommodate a request such as this, especially when it is asked politely and with an obvious desire to understand.

Josh also learned to clarify the meaning of what was said by asking, "Do you mean _____?" If Josh did not understand instructions even when they were repeated, he learned to ask the speaker if she could say the directions in another way. By politely asking, "Could you explain that in a different way?" Josh has found that most people are willing to try to rephrase their statements in order to have their instructions understood. These strategies have become more natural and automatic for Josh with repeated practice over time.

Advocating

Over the years, I have had to explain to Josh's teachers that if they do not allow him to have an adequate amount of time in which to respond, his flow of thought is disrupted and he has to start over again. Especially before Josh became proficient in the use of these strategies, his responses were labored and prolonged as he searched for words to express himself. If the listener interrupted or asked for clarification while Josh was still talking, Josh would hesitate and go back to the beginning of his comments and hope that the listener could discern the main points as Josh repeated them.

I have been guilty of interrupting Josh's thought processes many times, since he and I do not generally approach tasks at the same rate of speed. Waiting for Josh to answer is especially difficult when I talk to him on the phone, because I do not have the benefit of visual cues to help me determine if he is processing what I've said or if he's become distracted by extraneous activities near the phone. During one phone conversation I repeated my question to Josh, not even sure at that point if he was still on the phone. He told me "Hang on, Mom. My train of thought is still boarding." Okay, knowing that, I can wait!

There are still times when I talk to Josh and he does not answer even when he has clearly heard what I've said. When I ask him for a response, he sometimes seems surprised as if he's answered me in his head and just forgot to say it out loud. I remind him at those times that he needs to communicate some sort of response to let me and other people know he hears us. He has improved in this area, but it clearly still does not come naturally to him.

Interrupting

Many children get into the habit of interrupting others so they can tell about their own ideas without having to wait for a turn to talk. When a child is impulsive, it is even more difficult for them to wait their turn, and interrupting becomes part of the child's repertoire of communication strategies. I wanted Josh to be polite and demonstrate good manners, but he had so many ideas that he frequently interrupted to share them as they occurred to him.

To work on waiting for a turn to talk when I was conversing with someone else, I taught Josh to come up to me and touch my arm. That was his way of signaling me that he had something to say and wanted my attention. It did not disrupt the conversation I was engaged in with the other person, and was a quiet and unobtrusive way of getting my attention. I tried to respond to him quickly at a natural pause in the conversation, because I understood how difficult it was for him to wait quietly.

If Josh had an urgent need for my attention, then in addition to touching my arm he would say, "Excuse me." That was a more polite way of breaking into a conversation and was much more acceptable than running up and blurting out whatever was on his mind. It took much practice and discussion before Josh could discern what would be considered "urgent". Josh also had to practice repeatedly how to rest his hand on my arm rather than poke-poke-poking it or any other nearby body part within range! Gradually and with much work, Josh learned alternatives to interrupting.

Figures of Speech

Figurative language and proverbial statements present another challenge for the child who tends to take words literally. I learned that I could not say things like "There's a fork in the road" without going on to explain exactly what that meant. I deliberately taught my children the meanings of clichés, proverbial sayings, and figurative language. I incorporated that into their schooling as part of their language arts education. As they got older, I had each child select one cliché to learn each week, encouraging them to think of situations where the saying might be appropriately used.

As with many skills, the use of proverbial statements improves with practice. I try to incorporate them in our daily activities, so they are learned in natural contexts. Even misused figurative language can be a time of learning, and sometimes amusement.

When Beckie was eight years old, she was enjoying a snack and started to bounce on a therapy ball at the same time. I told her she needed to sit still while she ate, and could bounce some more after her snack. She sat quietly for about thirty seconds, and then absent-mindedly began bouncing again. This time I used her full name as I said "Rebecca! You may not bounce while you eat because you might choke. Now sit still on a chair until you are finished eating." She responded with "All right, Mom. You don't have to throw your top at me!" She meant, "Blow your top" but the tension diminished as I envisioned myself flinging my sweater toward her to get her to cease bouncing while she ate.

Personal Space

My daughter Beth is adept at many social skills. She understands nuances and implications of words and body language with an ease that allows her to adapt to new situations easily. Social interactions dictate the amount of physical distance to be left between people (on average, approximately three feet in our culture), and while children like Beth don't even have to think about it, some children have difficulty figuring out the expectations in this area.

The acceptable amount of personal space varies among different cultures, and most people automatically adapt to the accepted space for the culture in which they live. Through observation of others and feedback from personal experience, the average person will adapt to social norms in this area. For some individuals, however, the appropriate distance between conversation partners must be consciously thought about and practiced. The accepted space allowance for a given culture may not feel natural or comfortable to all members of the society.

I realized that personal space was an issue for Josh when he participated in team sports and his coaches would frequently say, "Josh! Get over here with the rest of the team!" Josh would be off a short distance away, out of range for any physical contact and inadvertent bumping by teammates. This coping strategy to avoid unpleasant or unexpected physical contact worked against him, though, because he often missed verbal directions and his lack of eye contact gave the impression (sometimes accurately) that he was not paying attention.

Josh needed a much larger area of personal space than most in order to feel comfortable. He did not always avoid physical contact, and was very physically affectionate with his family members. During play, at times he would even deliberately bump and crash into others. It seemed mainly that crowds and unpredictable physical contact were intimidating to him, and the larger the group, the more space he sought.

Maintaining a sizeable area of interpersonal space was counterproductive for Josh because he was less likely to be included in conversations and often had difficulty hearing instructions over the noise of the crowd. Josh often found interesting objects to engage his attention rather than attend to a speaker or coach. If the speaker was not directly facing him, Josh quickly gave up on trying to pay attention and found other things to occupy himself with until the situation changed. This led to more misunderstandings and frustration for both Josh and the group leaders.

As Josh and I role-played the appropriate distance for conversation in our culture, Josh struggled to figure out how close to stand to me. The accepted range of distance did not feel right to him much of the time. With much practice he has been able to approximate the accepted personal space during social exchanges, but Josh's natural tendency is to step back and enlarge the distance between himself and others. He has to force himself to remain in close proximity to others in a crowded area.

Josh's reluctance to remain physically close to others in a group led him to develop alternatives. He would find other activities that allowed him more room to move around freely, and would happily pursue those activities by himself. At the neighborhood swimming pool, rather than sit with a group of children until the rest period was over, Josh developed a route that he walked around the pool grounds. He walked hunched over, scanning the ground.

Some children who noticed Josh walking all alone called him unkind names, but Josh just ignored them. I realized that Josh enjoyed being alone sometimes, and that he was not lonely just because he was by himself. He always had things to think about, and he often found interesting bits of trash ("treasures") or coins during his walking route. Josh enjoyed both the opportunity to make discoveries and the space to move around without constraints or unanticipated physical contact with others.

Taking Conversational Turns

Conversation should be a two-way communication characterized by each person taking turns in the exchange. This has been a difficult skill for Josh to develop since he often misses subtle nonverbal cues and has a tendency to ramble on as he expresses himself. I have tried having Josh say one sentence, and then I say one, alternating in like fashion. Josh can do this in structured situations, but continues to experience difficulty generalizing the skill to spontaneous exchanges in conversations with others.

It is also a challenge for Josh to maintain a single topic of conversation. With his seemingly scattershot approach to conversation, he hits the target occasionally but often misses badly. To help develop this skill of staying on one topic, we practiced selecting items and saying three things about each item. We discussed movies and stories and talked about the main points of each. Many times Josh has difficulty recognizing the main ideas being presented. Sometimes a smaller detail that seems less consequential will grab Josh's attention to a greater extent than do the key ideas. It stimulates his imagination and he develops the ideas that occur to him.

Josh genuinely views things from a different perspective. It is not something he has to work at; he is genuinely a creative thinker. He is not bound by conventional ways of thinking, so something that seems to be a minor detail may have greater significance to Josh than the intended key ideas. Josh's incredibly creative way of approaching situations allows him to see possibilities I would miss. It also makes it difficult at times to follow his conversational development and his reasoning as it takes unpredictable twists and turns.

I have been told by a number of individuals that Josh thinks "outside the box", meaning he has an unconventional way of viewing things and solving problems. To those people, I often respond, "He doesn't even know there is a box!" I am very much conventional in my thinking and problem solving, and although I'd like to think it's a fairly big box, I am most certainly an "inside the box" kind of thinker. Josh's unique approach to tasks is rarely one I would have anticipated or come up with myself, but it is often better than my best attempt.

Josh's tendency to see things differently often leads to his proposing alternative ideas and ways to doing things. It is hard to remember that Josh is "wired" differently, so he is often perceived as being argumentative or contrary. We once considered giving Josh the nickname "Ford," because he always has "a better idea" just like the car company slogan claims it has in its advertising.

<u>Social Skills Strategies</u>
- **Talk about what others are talking about.**
- **Take turns talking and listening.**
- **Let people know you heard them – speak or gesture.**
- **Practice eye contact.**
- **Role play common situations.**
- **Practice appropriate body language and tone of voice.**

It helps Josh to talk out loud as he develops ideas. Unfortunately, he tends to monopolize conversations when he does this. He can also bore his listener without even realizing it, because he does not readily pick up on nonverbal cues. One such instance led to a family code phrase to let Josh know when he is not allowing his conversational partner to respond.

Josh has always enjoyed telling me about his Lego creations. Even as he explains them, new ideas occur to him on ways to improve or alter his projects. Once he hunted me down late in the evening when I was already tired and trying to get some work done before heading to bed. He came to me and asked if he could tell me about the Lego creation he had made. Knowing his tendency to go on and on, I told him he could tell me the three main features.

Josh enthusiastically plunged into a detailed explanation, barely pausing for breath as he spoke. As his description lengthened, I reminded him that he was only supposed to tell me three things. "Aw, Mom!" Josh protested as he pointed to one of the little Lego bumps. "I want to give you the bump-by-bump version!" We both had a good laugh about that, and still refer to the "bump-by-bump" way of describing something.

Coaching Through Scripts

When a child struggles with social interactions, relating to unfamiliar people can be challenging. It's a good idea to teach some familiar phrases to use to ease the pressure of determining what to say in new situations. Children can learn how to respond to social greetings and partings with the standard phrases typically used. Even children who are temperamentally shy or introverted can be taught the importance of responding to someone politely.

Introducing yourself, learning someone's name, and knowing how to respond to frequently asked questions are all skills that can be role played at home and practiced in other settings. A child may need assistance in thinking of good questions to ask to convey interest in another person.

It helps the struggling communicator to have a few memorized questions and phrases to use in new situations. Examples: "What's your name?", "Where do you work/go to school?" or "What do you like to do for fun?" These skills do not come naturally for everyone, but most of us can improve once we have suggestions on what to try and are given the opportunity to practice new skills.

Older Children

As Josh gets older and the expectations for social exchanges get more complicated, we have continued to work together in partnership. Josh knows that I like him and that I'm sincerely trying to help him, so he listens and tries my suggestions. It is a little more difficult for him to hear suggestions from his slightly younger sister, since she does not always make her opinions known in the most tactful way. I am aware that Josh is more easily embarrassed and is more self-conscious than when he was a young child. With that in mind, I coach him with even greater sensitivity and in private.

Since Josh is tall for his age, people often assume he is older than his true age. Expectations tend to change as children get older, and the children need to take more responsibility and advocate for themselves in social situations. Adults and other children expect older children to communicate adequately, without the assistance of their loving mothers or fathers. But parents can still coach their children and remind them to use good strategies, even intervening if it is necessary.

Following both successful and difficult communication attempts, I encourage Josh to think about what worked or didn't work for him. He is maturing and is ready to do some self-evaluation. If he realizes that a particular strategy worked well for him, he is likely to use it again in future encounters. My goal is never for him to be dependent on me, but to help him develop his own abilities, as he is increasingly able.

When Josh begins to think about his own social interaction goals and how to accomplish them, he also begins to accept responsibility for the outcome of his actions and any changes that need to be made. My role becomes more one of listener and mentor, providing suggestions and guidance to help keep him moving forward.

Today, at age fourteen, Josh engages in social interactions with a greater facility than would have seemed possible after seeing his earlier struggles. Now when he meets someone for the first time he makes eye contact, shakes hands, and verbally greets the person. He responds to other's interaction attempts, and asks for clarification in ways that now seem natural to him. He initiates interaction in more appropriate ways and has improved in his ability to keep a conversation going. It is gratifying now to hear many people comment that Josh is very well behaved and polite.

While watching a movie recently, Josh observed a man's awkward and ineffective attempts to communicate with his son. Josh sadly shook his head and stated with empathy, "That poor guy has a hard time with social skills." The fact that Josh even noticed and identified the difficulty shows his immense progress in the area of social communication.

Certain aspects of communicating may never feel natural to Josh, but with motivation and practice he can continue to develop basic skills that will serve him throughout his lifetime. Even when there are foundational components of communication that have not developed naturally, there is still hope for improvement as individual skills are taught and consciously exercised. Successful communication can be extremely rewarding and is worth the effort it takes to achieve it.

Josh Boring, age 14
Beth Boring, age 13

<u>Chapter 11 – Brain-Based Teaching and Learning</u>

The brain is an amazing organ. Researchers have discovered much about the way the brain functions, and I find the information fascinating. What interests me the most is how brain performance impacts learning. I want to use known information about the brain to make my teaching compatible with the optimal ways students learn and remember new information.

What The Brain Likes

Many people find that they are more alert and can think more clearly when they are standing up or able to move around.[4] When I began teaching my children, I had them sit at desks. Over time, I have realized that they could be more productive when allowed to move or stand. Working at a drafting table is an excellent option for a student who likes to stand while working. The height of the table can be adjusted for comfort, and the student can either stand or use a stool while working. Some stools swivel so the student can easily move from side to side.

The brain needs water to be hydrated for optimal functioning.[5] For that reason, I encourage my children to drink water while they are doing their schoolwork. In order to avoid having them frequently interrupting their

[4] Sousa, David. (2001). <u>How the Brain Learns: A Classroom Teacher's Guide.</u> California: Corwin Press, Inc.
[5] Dennison, P. & G. Dennison. (1994). <u>Brain Gym, Teacher's Edition Revised.</u> (p.24) California: Edu-Kinesthetics, Inc.

work to get a drink, I allow them to keep a sports bottle filled with ice water in their work area. Sports bottles are advantageous because they are not likely to spill if they are tipped over, since they have lids with straws or closable spouts.

I provide healthy snacks for my children to eat while they are working. Hunger distracts them, and when they are distracted they are not in an optimal state for learning. I choose snacks that do not require much preparation and are not inherently messy.

The smell of peppermint is an alerting aroma, so I try to keep a supply of hard peppermint candies around to use during school time.[6] The children like the peppermints, and I encourage them to have one, especially when doing work that requires focused concentration. I just make sure they are in a chair and able to sit still, and have them brush their teeth often!

Emotions At Work

When Beckie is nervous I can always tell because her hands stray up to her mouth. Many people like Beckie find it calming to have something in their mouths to suck or chew on. Beckie likes crunchy or chewy foods the best, and I try to keep chewing gum available for times when she is not hungry but still feels the need to have something in her mouth. The sensation of chewing the gum seems to help her to focus and feel less tense.

---

[6]Maxwell-Hudson, Clare. (1994). <u>Aromatherapy Massage</u>. (p.31) New York: DK Publishing, Inc.

One of my favorite brain-friendly teaching tips is to involve the students' emotions whenever possible during teaching. Experiencing emotions can actually cause chemical changes in the brain that make the experience more likely to be remembered.[7] Any strong emotion can promote memorization, but of course I try to appeal to positive emotions as I teach.

I like to use storytelling to involve emotions. I may read from a book or just tell a story, with or without props. My children gain insight into various characters and the impact of the characters' actions and decisions on themselves and others. When the story truly engages them, they identify and share some of the emotions of the characters. Role-playing is another fun and effective way to make a point memorable through storytelling.

Using Color

When I add an illustration during a lesson, even if it is only a simple drawing on a dry erase board, my children typically remember the information. I encourage them to make their own illustrations, too, since that will also aid memorization. It does not require great artistic ability, since even a stick figure can help to make the point being taught more memorable. This is an especially effective technique for strong visual learners, who tend to remember visual images with ease.

---

[7] Hannaford, Carla. (1995). <u>Smart Moves.</u> (pp.50-69). Virginia: Great Ocean Publishers.

Using colors to facilitate learning is also very useful to aid in learning.[8] It is easier to remember what is seen in color, and colors can be used to help organize materials. Some students find it helpful to have a different color folder for each subject area. I have even used different colors of lined notebook paper to help my children organize their work by subject. The contrast provided by utilizing various colors makes illustrations and written material more interesting and more likely to be recalled later.

Keys to Brain-Compatible Learning
• *Water*
• *Movement*
• *Color*
• *Music*
• *Emotions*
• *Interaction*

Active Involvement

Any time a child is actively engaged in the learning process, the information is more likely to be retained. One way to increase involvement is to have the student verbalize what they are learning. This helps to bridge the gap between what the child knows and what the child is able to express adequately. As the child talks out loud, she learns to organize her thoughts in a coherent manner. It solidifies her thinking and helps her to

---

[8] Vitale, Barbara. (1982). <u>Unicorns Are Real</u>. (p. 67). California: Jalmar Press.

pinpoint any areas that remain unclear to her. As a teacher, it helps me to clarify what areas the student is understanding or having difficulties with and can help me identify areas needing further instruction. Children who love to talk appreciate the opportunity to use this strategy!

A similar technique to promote memorization is called sub-vocalizing. Sub-vocalizing is basically saying the information to oneself rather than actually speaking out loud. It is a technique many people use when needing to remember information such as a phone number. As I say the information to myself over and over, I am keeping it in my short-term memory. I might continue to sub-vocalize until I write the information down, no longer need the information, or actually have it memorized and stored in my long-term memory.

Sub-vocalizing is a useful technique for memorizing information in any subject area. Younger students can use this strategy when practicing math facts and memorizing spelling words. Older students can sub-vocalize with vocabulary terms or events in history. It is an effective technique that promotes focused attention and memorization, and can be used throughout a lifetime.

The brain easily retains and accesses information that is understood, familiar, and used frequently. For this reason, it helps to connect known information to new information when introducing novel material.[9] I try to make an association between a concept my children

[9] Buzan, Tony. (1974). Use Both Sides of Your Brain. (p.15) New York: E.P.Dutton.

already know and the new information I am presenting. I have them recall a familiar idea and then expand on it to include new information. For example, I will review a story we have read and then point out ways that the author was attempting to persuade the reader. Following that discussion, I teach my children methods for persuasive writing. Having an example in mind helps them grasp the concepts even when they have not attempted such a task previously.

Using Music

It may be helpful to allow your children to listen to classical instrumental music while they work. This helps block out some of the background noises and improves concentration. Play it at a volume that is audible but not distracting. Classical music with 55-70 beats per minute matches the brain's pattern when it is in a relaxed, alert state. This state is optimal for learning and remembering new information. Examples of selections that are appropriate for this purpose include music by Bach, Handel, and Mozart.[10]

The LIND Institute[11] has developed techniques for using scientifically selected classical music to promote learning, creative thinking, relaxation, and memorization. Their strategies are designed to be compatible with scientific findings on certain aspects of brain functioning.

---

[10] Andersen, Ole, Marcy Marsh, & Dr. Arthur Harvey. (1999). <u>Learn With The Classics</u>. California: LIND Institute.
[11] For more information visit www.lind-institute.com

I am no expert on the brain and its functions, but I have benefited by the work of others and the information that has become available in the area of brain compatible learning. The suggested tips are simple and inexpensive to incorporate regardless of curriculum or individual learning and teaching styles. It is worth the time and effort to try different approaches to presenting material, since it benefits both teachers and students when techniques promote successful learning.

Beth Boring   Age 13

<u>Chapter 12 – Adapting and Modifying Curriculum</u>

Teaching different students with varying abilities and approaches to learning is challenging even for the most experienced teacher. When a teacher has a specific curriculum that must be used with all students, the challenge increases.

I have had many conversations with disappointed home educators who bought packaged curriculum and then found that it wasn't working well for their child. Sometimes people end up buying several different programs for the same subject area in an attempt to find a good match for their child's ability and learning style.

Like these educators, I have had the experience of buying curriculum only to discover that the materials and suggested instructional methods were not effective for teaching my students. The costs of buying additional curriculum quickly add up in terms of expense as well as frustration. I try to find ways to supplement and change the materials I already have rather than replacing them entirely.

Observe The Students

If part of the difficulty in teaching is due to the distractibility of the students, there are a number of simple changes that can be done to help. First, try to determine the types of things that are most distracting for your child. Is she highly visual and needing to look around if there is motion or activity nearby? Does he seem to hear every little sound and react to what he hears? Does his sense of touch make it difficult for your child to comfortably settle down to work?

Observe your child in the areas of visual, auditory, and tactile responses throughout the day and in a variety of settings. Ask your child what they are thinking and feeling when you see them reacting in certain ways. Your child may have a combination of responses indicating distractibility in several areas, and if she can explain or describe what she experiences you can better determine methods for helping overcome or compensate for these issues.

Don't Be A Slave To Curriculum

The more insight I have into the way my children learn, the better I am able to adjust my expectations and find ways to alter curriculum to make it work for me. I read the publisher's suggested methods for utilizing the materials, and then decide if that is the best approach for me to use with my children. I use the instructor's manuals and the materials themselves to get ideas, and then I make changes to the curriculum to maximize its usefulness to my students.

I rarely entirely abandon curriculum once I have purchased it. There are aspects about the materials that were appealing enough to persuade me to buy it in the first place, and there are usually at least portions of it that I still want to use. It is also rare for me to use curriculum exactly as suggested in the teacher's manual. I modify the material to meet my students' needs, and I adapt the ways in which I teach and the students respond.

What's Your Style?

One of the biggest changes I have had to make is to adjust my own style of teaching to fit the ways my children learn. It was not just a matter of figuring out their preferred mode for learning certain types of subjects, but really involved how they approached thinking and learning in general.

It took me a few years to figure out that Josh was the kind of learner who needed to see the whole picture and then look at the individual pieces that made up the whole. Josh needed to see where I was heading with a lesson, so he could understand the overall point of the lesson and how the steps along the way contributed to the final product. He is the kind of student who needs to know "What is the point, and why do I need to know this now?"

Once I knew that Josh was the kind of student who looked for the big picture and was not as interested in details, I tried to make sure he understood why we were doing the assignments and what the end result would be when they were completed. When I did not explain the goals sufficiently, Josh was more resistant to doing the work because he did not see the importance of it.

My own preferred style both for teaching and for learning is to advance in a sequential manner, starting at the beginning and following a linear progression to the conclusion. I like to finish what I start before moving on to another subject area. Whereas Josh loves experimenting, possibilities, risk-taking, and alternatives, I like details, predictability, and structure. In other words, Josh and I could not be much more different in our approaches to tasks.

My way of learning did not work for Josh, and just led to frustration for us both. Beth could learn from my step-by-step way of teaching, but fortunately she could also adapt to learn alongside Josh as I made changes in how I presented some subjects. In order to truly connect with Josh as a teacher to a student, there were a number of alterations I needed to make.

Although Josh needed to see the big picture, he had difficulty figuring out the steps needed to reach a long-term goal. He understood what the end product should be, but could not identify the smaller details that would help him attain the final result. His tendency was to procrastinate and then rush to get his work done at the last minute. His inability to plan left him struggling to break longer assignments down into manageable parts.

In addition to helping my students learn how to break down larger, long-range assignments into more manageable tasks, at times I have to show them how to break down a single problem or task into smaller steps. For example, Beth was intimidated by the thought of doing long division problems. She looked at sample problems and was convinced it would be too hard for her. When I went through a division problem with her, and pointed out what I was doing at each step, she began to relax. Once she realized that I was using addition, multiplication, and subtraction facts that she already knew herself, the idea of division was not as intimidating as it had been at first. She just needed to approach it a step at a time.

I try to deliver instruction to my children in a way that fits their preferred learning style. Josh is strongly visual, Beth learns through auditory methods, and Beckie is definitely a tactile learner. I aim for having them work in their natural strength areas about 80% of the time. This will help them experience success and avoid some of the frustrations that occur when they have to expend energy and effort to work in a non-preferred mode.

I still instruct my children in ways that will force them to develop some skills in areas that do not come naturally to them. Just because Josh is strong as a visual learner does not mean he can neglect his listening skills. Beth will have to visually analyze graphs and charts, even though she would prefer to learn through discussions. Beckie will not always have objects to touch to help her understand various topics. I want my children to have some compensatory skills for times when they are presented with information in different ways than they would choose for themselves.

Teachable Moments…Or Not!

Josh continues to have difficulty in this area. He knows what he wants but is not sure how to get there. I look for practical ways to help him see the steps that will lead him to achieving his goals. Josh once gave me a wonderful teaching opportunity as we were leaving his orthodontist's office. We left the building and walked across the parking lot toward our van. Parked next to it was a shiny red pick-up truck that looked brand new. Josh gazed admiringly at the truck, and then said, "Mom, when I'm an adult I want to have a truck like that."

I could tell Josh was impressed by the looks of the truck, so I thought it was a "teachable moment" for him. I responded to his statement with, "Josh, did you know a truck like that costs a lot of money?"

"No, Mom. I didn't know that."

I eagerly pointed out the facts. "Well, trucks like that are expensive, and if you want one someday you will need to have a job that pays you well so that you can afford it. In order to get a good-paying job, you need a good education. And if you want a good education, Josh, you're going to have to start working a little harder on your schoolwork."

By now we were driving back home. I was congratulating myself on presenting a logical explanation to Josh that would appeal to him and surely persuade him of the value of hard work and a good education. I glanced at Josh and could tell by his lowered head and his silence that he was considering all the things I had said. Finally, Josh raised his head, sighed deeply, and sadly replied, "Guess I'll get a motorcycle." So much for that teachable moment!

Same Curriculum, Different Output

I frequently adapt the way my children can respond to the information they are learning. The curriculum may call for a written response, but I make modifications based on time constraints and individual differences. Sometimes I let my children answer the questions orally. This demonstrates to me that they comprehend the material, and allows me to expand and provide further information if necessary. Allowing them to answer orally instead of by writing generally takes less time. Another benefit is that by voicing their thoughts they have practiced organizing and expressing ideas.

Especially For Writing

I also modify some writing tasks by allowing the children to dictate their responses as I write them down. I used this approach with Josh when he was younger, because I discovered that when I had him write his own stories he would use very basic, simple sentences. He also was careful to use short words that he knew how to spell so he wouldn't have to go back and make corrections! Since he disliked paper and pencil work when it did not include drawing, he did the least amount of work possible and it did not reflect what I thought he was truly capable of doing.

When Josh dictated stories for me to write down, he used long sentences with incredible descriptions. His mastery of the complexities of language and his developing vocabulary were evident. Once he was freed from the demands of actually writing on paper, his ideas were freely expressed. I still had him do some writing activities, because that was a valuable and necessary skill for him to develop. I just allowed him alternatives at times so that he could complete his work in a way that was more appealing to him.

Beckie also prefers to express herself in ways other than traditional paper and pencil tasks. When she was younger, I would sometimes take turns with her as we wrote down her answers. At times I let her draw a picture and then tell me about it. Beckie has done art projects, made up songs, and acted out skits to demonstrate to me that she is learning. All of these are ways of adapting the output required by commercial curricula. There are many creative ways for a child to demonstrate her growing knowledge.

Especially for Math

Even children who are strong visual learners, if they have a tendency to be impulsive while working, may still make careless errors although they understand the concepts being taught. I found this to be true for Josh, who had a good understanding of math but often made careless errors in his calculations. He did not take the time to carefully line up his columns of numbers when he performed mathematical functions. The result was that his numbers would tend to drift into the wrong columns. This was not an area of difficulty that would be solved by trying another curriculum, since he would be doing calculations with any program I selected.

Instead, I made a simple accommodation for Josh. I provided him with graph paper and instructed him in how to write one digit in each square so that the columns of numbers lined up properly. His accuracy immediately improved. Graph paper is available in a variety of sizes, so I selected one that was a good fit with Josh's fine motor skills and developmental abilities.

As Josh got a little older, I switched from using graph paper to using lined notebook paper. He started each lesson with two sheets of paper. One was for writing his answers down and the other was for working out the math problems. I turned the problem-solving paper sideways, so Josh could use the lines on it as columns for the numbers. This helped Josh keep the numbers lined up so that he did not miss problems he truly knew how to do.

Josh likes to get his schoolwork done so he has time for other interests. It frustrates him to have to repeat work he has already done or do math problems that he already knows how to do. It feels like a waste of time to him, and although my tendency is to want to do entire lessons as they are written in the textbook I needed to modify Josh's assignments.

Sometimes I would have Josh just do the odd-numbered math problems. If he got them all correct, he was proving that he understood the concept being practiced. The next day he might do the even-numbered problems, with the understanding that we would do the rest of the problems if he needed more practice. Modifying the size of the assignment can be done with any curriculum.

"On" Days and "Off" Days

My students have days when they are doing well and the work flows easily. There are also days when everything about schoolwork seems hard. As a teacher as well as a mom, I have to adapt the amount of support I give my children. Some days they need more personal assistance and I need to remain in close proximity as they work. At those times, I let the answering machine pick up rather than answer the phone myself, because I know my children will lose their focus if I am not physically present. I also need to offer more encouragement on those "off" days, and discern when it is time to move on to a new activity or be finished with schoolwork for the day.

Varying the time allowed for an activity is another way to adapt curriculum. Josh has difficulty with timed tests because he is distractible and he has a poor sense regarding the passage of time. For several years I had a certified teacher do a portfolio assessment of Josh's work. I did not have him take a standardized achievement test because I felt that a timed test would not accurately reflect Josh's true abilities. The first time he did take a timed achievement test, I hired a certified teacher to come to my house and administer the test in private so Josh would have fewer distractions than in a group setting.

There are days when I anticipate completing a lesson within a certain period of time, and I find that more time is needed than I originally planned for my children to get their work finished. This is a matter of individual differences, and would be a factor no matter what curriculum I selected. Occasionally my children will complete a task in less time than I expected, and we are able to move through material more rapidly.

Simple Instructional Accommodations

- *Know the student's and your own learning styles.*
- *Break down assignments into manageable parts for students.*
- *Allow alternative responses (drawing, oral answers, dictate answers, etc.)*
- *Use creative expression to keep students engaged – projects, skits, etc.*
- *Use lined or graph paper for math.*
- *Give shorter assignments.*
- *Acknowledge the "on" days and "off" days – adjust expectations.*
- *Vary the time allowed for completing assignments.*
- *Give more personal support when needed.*
- *Utilize technology.*
- *Experiment with seating and lighting.*
- *Involve as many senses as possible.*

Having The Students Teach Others

One of the most effective ways to encourage learning with my children is to put them in the role of teacher. When they were younger, I would present information and then ask them to pretend they were the teacher and to teach me what they were learning. As

Josh and Beth got older, I would encourage them to help teach Beckie and other younger children some of the material they were learning.

When Josh and Beth are able to teach others, they feel more confident in their own understanding of the subject matter. Presenting the information to others in a way they can understand engages their thought processes as they determine how to explain and demonstrate what they have learned.

As students teach material they are learning, they develop the ability to rephrase instructions that are not readily understood the first time, and they recognize the need to be patient and encouraging with struggling learners. This is a quick way to get the students actively involved in learning and allows for a brief assessment of their understanding as the adult teacher observes them. Having children teach others is a useful strategy that can be used with any available curriculum.

Utilizing Technology

Josh and Beckie may never gain great pleasure by writing with pencil and paper. Yet they have such interesting ideas to share I have been determined to find ways for them to express their ideas in written form. Using the computer and keyboarding skills has been a successful option for my children.

The computer is more interactive and involves more of the senses than traditional writing programs do and, because this is true, the computer keeps their attention for longer periods of time. Written mistakes are easily corrected without the need for cumbersome erasing, and Josh can use spell check applications to help catch spelling errors.

Josh loves gadgets, and uses a Franklin Spelling Ace® to check his spelling. He knows how to use a dictionary, but becomes frustrated with the time it takes to find a word. He already knows what part of speech it is and what the word means. He just needs to know how to spell it. The Franklin Spelling Ace® is about the size of a hand-held calculator, and when the student enters a word it provides a list of possible words close to that spelling. Josh can usually recognize the correct spelling of the word he is looking for, although he has trouble coming up with the spelling on his own.

I believe it will be beneficial to my children to learn to use computers comfortably and competently. I also value the ability to type accurately and rapidly, and have been working with my children to help them develop their skills in that area. I often supplement textbook learning with computer programs that offer video clips or other features that are difficult to achieve through the use of textbooks alone.

Be Creative and Experiment

There are numerous factors in any setting that can be explored and adapted to impact learning. Try different levels of brightness in lighting, for example. Some students prefer to study and read with just a soft light from a lamp. Subdued lighting seems more relaxing to them, and is conducive to learning. Others prefer very bright lighting and feel less alert when the lighting is dimmed.

Seating arrangements offer another area for exploring options. Some students like sitting in chairs at a desk or table, but others learn better when they are relaxed in a beanbag chair or other alternative location. Some students are able to function best while sitting on a therapy ball or with a sitting disk on a chair.

With a little creativity and determination, teachers can find ways to modify curriculum and the learning environment to suit the learners' needs. My best leads on how to do that have come from the students themselves. As I listen to their ideas and observe them as they work, I begin to see with greater clarity the many ways they think and respond. When I find methods that appeal to their unique approaches to learning, schoolwork becomes more satisfying for all involved.

Beth Boring   Age 13

<u>Chapter 13 – Adults Need Breaks Too!</u>

Since I was often in bed soon after my young children went to bed for the night, I rarely had moments of solitude or quiet reflection. I have always been able to think and concentrate best without interruption and when it is quiet around me. Yet quiet and solitude are rare luxuries at my house. When the noise and activities seem to be continuous, I find myself feeling increasingly agitated and irritable as I strain to concentrate and prioritize my activities.

Escaping the Noise

Scott, on the other hand, is not bothered by noise. In fact, he produces quite a bit of noise himself through his electronic equipment. When Scott is relaxing, he likes engaging in an activity on the computer and listening to the radio at the same time. He keeps the volume loud enough that he can move from room to room and still hear what he is playing. He enjoys listening to music at a volume level that is uncomfortable for me. The children often have to repeat what they have said to him because he screens out some sounds to attend to others, usually giving attention to whatever is the loudest or most insistent sound.

I begin to twitch inside after a time of being bombarded with noise. I get to a point of agitation and have to eliminate some of the noises before I can continue on with other tasks. When I am involved with routine activities that require little conscious thought, I can tolerate noise better. When I need to concentrate and think deeply, however, I need a fairly quiet environment.

Pursuit of Solitude

When the children were very young, I tried getting up earlier in the morning so that I could have some time of solitude to prepare for the day. This may be an option for some people. In my case, living in an old house with creaking floors and steps made it impossible to move about silently when I arose in the morning. As soon as my children heard me up and about, they got up to join me. It did not matter how early I got up, the children always heard me and awoke. Once Josh was in an upright position he was fully awake and on the go, and clearly he felt more rested than I did. The result was that my day started even earlier than usual, I was still tired, and I still did not obtain the solitude I so desired.

In another attempt to obtain this solitude, I instituted short periods of quiet time for the children in the afternoon. Beth would often nap, but Josh genuinely did not need to sleep and just played quietly. During this time I tried to plan, return phone calls, or complete any other task requiring greater concentration than I was able to achieve in a noisy atmosphere. I found I was able to get much more done in less time when I could work without interruptions and distractions.

I had to help Josh find quiet activities to do both during our daytime rest period and at night when he wasn't feeling tired enough to sleep. When I insisted he stay in bed, he felt lonely and restless because he genuinely wasn't sleepy. He could easily have stayed up with his Dad and me until we were ready to turn in for the night, but since we needed some adult time, we had to come up with alternatives.

I allowed Josh to play with his Legos® or other small toys beside his bed until he was ready to sleep. I had to institute a "no dumping" rule, because the sound of Legos® being poured from a bucket would wake up his sisters. Josh learned to sort through his toys quietly, and would climb into bed when he was finally ready to sleep. I learned to never walk barefoot into Josh's room to check on him at night, because stepping on Legos® is very painful!

Change of Environment

Besides needing a little quiet time during each day, I found it extremely helpful when I could leave the children home with their Dad and have an hour or two to myself. I did simple things such as going to the library or taking a walk. Being alone gave me time to gather my thoughts, pray, and have a short reprieve from the constant flow of activities that demanded my attention at home. I could get much more done in less time when I was not needing to attend to small children.

I did not need to spend much time away from home, but even a few hours a week made a difference to me. I returned home refreshed and revitalized, feeling better able to do all that I had committed to doing. Getting the time away was truly an investment because it helped me to keep my perspective and relieved some of the effects of stress and weariness that built up over time. Taking even a short break allowed me time to recharge and relax.

My children learned that having time with their Dad when I was away could be quite entertaining and enjoyable. Scott's style of relating is very different from mine and the children relished having his attention. Scott gained a greater appreciation for the energy and attention required in caring for our young children, and better understood my need for occasional breaks. The children learned that with Dad, you had to ask for meals when you were hungry because they didn't just appear like they did when Mom was home!

Time As A Couple

When the children were very young, it was also a challenge to nurture my marriage. As much as Scott and I loved our children, the frustrations of constant demands and the uncertainty of how to parent an atypical child created stress. Additionally, I had to undergo two sinus surgeries when Beth was six months old and Josh was not yet two years old. The sickness, medical bills, and slow recovery all contributed to the pressures on our marriage and family.

Scott and I could not financially afford to go out very often, and we did not have many relatives nearby who were able to watch our children for us so that we could have consistent time alone together. Josh was a handful even for the most experienced babysitter, so we usually stayed home and grabbed what time we could when the children were in bed for the night. Please notice that I didn't say the children were asleep, but they were in bed! This was clearly not the ideal way to maintain our marriage relationship, but it was all we were able to manage at that time in our lives.

Mothers Still Have Adult Needs

During the first several years after I became a mother, I found I no longer had time for activities I had previously enjoyed. I no longer made craft items or read books for enjoyment, and although I missed those activities I had difficulty figuring out how to reintroduce them into my full and busy life. I sensed that somehow I needed to add back at least some of the activities I had previously enjoyed without compromising the care of my family.

I satisfied my need for creative expression by exploring art activities and making various crafts with my children. Josh, as usual, always had ideas about how the activities could be done differently. I decided to give him the opportunity to use his creativity with full expression in his art projects, and let him try his ideas to the extent that space and materials would allow. Josh became less reluctant to handle various textures, and at the same time, Beckie managed to turn every art project into a head-to-toe experience, usually requiring much soap and water at its conclusion. Beth couldn't wait to show her Dad the finished project and she always enjoyed the process of creating art.

It took me quite awhile longer to figure out a way to add reading back into my life. I read daily to my children, and it was time that we all enjoyed. On the rare occasion when I sat down to read a book by myself, however, my children quickly snuggled up next to me. They would confidently hold forth their books for me to read to them. I didn't want to squelch their love of books or their desire to be with me, so I would read their books to them and put my own book aside.

One day as I was fixing dinner and listening to the radio, a thought struck me. I could be listening to audio books while engaging in everyday tasks such as cooking, cleaning, and laundry. A trip to the library and the purchase of a portable cassette player with headphones, and I was once again enjoying the literary works I could no longer sit down to read. Since then, I have been listening to books on tape without having to carve additional time into my schedule, since I listen while I do other work. The day may come when I can again sit down and turn the pages of an actual book, but until that time I will continue to enjoy audio books.

Healthy Habits

I have heard that it takes much more energy to parent a hyperactive child than a child without hyperactivity. All children require time and energy, and a child with special needs requires even more. It is not unusual for the home schooling parent to work so hard at helping her children that she neglects to guard some healthy time for herself. Some children are by nature more demanding than others, and sometimes those demands can seem relentless. When a parent who is not high-energy is paired with a hyperactive child, the demands seem even more exhausting.

I believe that adults need to establish some healthy habits for themselves in order to be able to continue an endeavor such as home schooling over a long period of time. Without adequate time for relaxation and developing or maintaining supportive relationships, feelings of isolation and discouragement grow. The fatigue that can accompany lack of exercise or an inadequate amount of sleep also makes it difficult to sustain the effort to home school over time.

Some people think that taking the time to meet your own individual needs is a selfish pursuit. It is not my intent to encourage selfishness, but establishing healthy habits is in the best interest of the entire family. Everyone has needs, and taking the time for exercise, fellowship, and personal development is going to help keep the necessary balance in life. For example, a home schooling parent may suffer physical ailments or feelings of discouragement to such an extent that continuing homeschooling appears overwhelming.

Many homeschoolers reach a point where they are so exhausted after years of home schooling that they feel they can no longer educate their children at home and enroll their children in school. This is certainly not the case for every family who decides it is time for their children to attend school outside the home. However, it does seem to be a major contributing factor for many families who feel drained by the time and energy demands of home schooling. The work required, especially if the children are resistant or lack motivation, makes it seem that homeschooling is no longer feasible or worth the cost. Taking steps to ensure breaks and pursue the necessary support for the teaching parent is critical for the well being of the family and to prevent homeschooling burnout.

Children need focused attention from their parents, and are persistent in pursuing it. Most adults strive to give the needed time and resources to their children, sometimes in excess of what the children truly need. Wise parents will set an example for their children as they maintain healthy habits for themselves and enjoy the benefits of a life lived in proper balance.

Beth Boring   age 13

<u>Chapter 14 – Developing the Strengths</u>

Josh's struggles were so apparent that they were impossible to ignore. Only slightly less apparent were some incredible strengths and areas of gifting that Josh displayed. One of my primary reasons in deciding to homeschool was to ensure that Josh would not feel inferior to others due to his differences. By homeschooling we could individualize his education to facilitate his success. I also wanted Beth to learn at her own pace, see herself accurately, and not feel superior for her lack of academic struggles. Beckie also reaped the benefits of this approach.

Viewing Yourself Accurately

An accurate view of oneself is part of a well-rounded education, and I was determined that all my children, especially Josh, would perceive themselves in a truthful manner. As a family, we acknowledged the areas of weakness, knowing that we all have weaknesses as well as strengths. Just as some weaknesses are more obvious than others, some strengths are more readily visible even upon casual inspection.

Many schools now incorporate character education into the curriculum. Home schooling has provided us with an excellent arena for character development as we have learned to appreciate the abilities God has given us and enjoy the differences in our areas of strength. We have worked on perseverance, thankfulness, and honesty in the natural context of our family dynamics. We have practiced forgiveness and humility and have seen the effects of our bad attitudes on those we love. We have addressed character issues as they arise, because we recognize patterns of behavior that occur in our daily interactions with each other.

Find Areas of Ability and Talent

Although Josh needed help to accomplish tasks that came easily to others, it would not have been in his best interest to allow him to view himself as incapable or as a victim of his disorder. To combat this, we worked to identify and develop Josh's talents. Since he was exceptionally creative and loved to draw, we enrolled him in art classes where he excelled and experienced success.

Josh also had a great deal of physical energy, but expressed little interest in most sports since they involved fast-paced group activities that were overwhelming to him. I had heard that martial arts were helpful in developing focus and concentration in ADHD children, and although the classes are taught in groups the skills are practiced individually as well. I later learned that martial arts is effective in promoting coordination because of the cross-body movements involved, and I interviewed an excellent instructor who was willing to work with me in helping Josh succeed. Josh has progressed at his own pace and is proud of his hard-won accomplishments in martial arts.

Beckie does better in group settings than Josh did at her age, but she has always been very intimidated by competition and the thought of letting her team down. Since she also has excess energy, I encouraged her to develop her swimming skills where she competes as a part of a team but also works to improve her own individual times. She has been fortunate to have some coaches who are patient with her and accept her idiosyncrasies as they help her develop her skills. I have also taught her that losing can be a valuable experience, and that no one can win every time. I am not sure I have completely convinced Beckie yet, but she is less reluctant to compete now than when she was younger.

Beckie also demonstrated at a young age the ability to hear a melody and sing it back. I applauded her enthusiasm for singing, and also had her begin piano lessons to further develop her musical abilities. Since Beckie has been so responsive to music, we memorize information through songs and familiar tunes. At times Beckie will make up songs to help her express ideas.

Beckie and Beth also show a propensity for drawing and other artistic expression, so they take art classes as well. They can happily explore with crafts for hours, and even made an elaborate artsy mask without my help this year. Each child has her own style for art, so another's talent does not intimidate her and she feels comfortable asking for and offering suggestions.

Beth has no particular academic struggles, but is easily hurt and very sensitive to what others think of her. To develop her character, I have worked on getting Beth to tell herself the truth in any given circumstance. She needs to know that she is still valuable and loved, even when others are displeased or angry at something she has done. She must learn that she will not always please others with her decisions, and that she must be strong enough to make hard decisions and take a stand anyway.

Being Realistic

Josh knows that I speak at workshops and share stories about him, but it does not bother him in the least. I think this is because he knows I love him and he is willing for me to share information that might be helpful to others. We've learned some things along the way, and we don't want to keep it to ourselves.

Once after spending a day at a homeschooling conference and presenting several workshops, my husband offered to take our family out to dinner so I could rest up a little before the next busy day. Once we arrived at the restaurant, Josh was even more wiggly and active than usual. I wearily reminded him to remain upright in the booth we were sitting in as we waited for our food to arrive. Josh kept up an uncharacteristic animated volley of chatter until I finally asked him what was going on with him. "I'm just giving you more material for your workshops, Mom!" he informed me with his most charming smile.

I think Josh has a realistic view of himself. He knows that some tasks are harder for him than they are for most people, but he also knows he can easily do some things that are challenging to others. He has a balanced and accurate perspective. As he was growing up, he frequently heard me telling him the things I noticed he could do well. I also had him verbalize what he was good at, so he would not dwell on his struggles. It took time, but Josh got to the point where I could ask him what he was good at and he could answer without hesitation or the need to stop and think about it. It became a part of how he thought about himself, and it has never left him.

Different Yet Equal

When Josh was in first grade, we found out he needed to wear glasses because his eyes were going out of focus after a few seconds of close-up work. He was supposed to wear the glasses anytime we did academic work, and this upset him. We also found out at the same time that Josh was colorblind, and he had hopes of being an artist one day!

When we got home from the optometrist appointment, Josh came to me in tears, and asked why all these things were wrong with him. He had ADHD, needed glasses, couldn't see colors accurately, and struggled with schoolwork. His slightly younger sister had none of these difficulties and he didn't understand why he did and she didn't.

I had anticipated that the time would come when Josh would ask questions such as this, but I had no well-prepared answers for him. I simply told him what I knew in my heart to be true, that God had created Josh for a reason, and that he was exactly what God had intended him to be. I didn't know why different people had different struggles, but I believed God would help us with everything we needed. I also pointed out that not everything came easily to his sister, and that he had strengths that she did not.

I reassured Josh that I not only loved him, but I liked him as well. I told him that we would keep working together to overcome obstacles and that I believed he was capable of doing great things. I knew it would be hard work, but I also truly believed he was worth it and I told him so. I promised never to give up on him, and that I would always be cheering for him.

I don't know how much of what I said that night really penetrated Josh's heart, but he seemed comforted and rarely compared himself to others again. He seems to have accepted what he's been given, both the strengths and the weaknesses. He recognizes both as equally valid components that help comprise his identity. He knows who he is, and he accepts that.

Josh Boring, age 14

Chapter 15 – The Journey Continues

As I continue parenting and teaching my children, I realize that there will always be issues that baffle me and areas where I feel inadequate. I will never be able to cover all the material in all the school subject areas to the fullest extent possible. I will struggle to teach my children desirable character traits, even as I struggle with my own character weaknesses.

I know I will continue to pray for guidance and wisdom, because God understands my children even when I do not. I will never give up on helping my children grow into the adults they were intended to be. Perhaps in time the direction they must go will become clearer.

I think that one of the most important ways we can invest in our children is to have a vision for their future and impart that vision to them. When I talk to my children about possible activities I envision them doing in the future, they begin to think about those possibilities themselves. God has given each of them areas of gifting and natural abilities that could lead them into a variety of opportunities and situations.

I want my children to enjoy the stages of life they are in now, and not be in a hurry to get older so they can do more adult activities. There are plenty of activities that they can do at any age, and if they are too focused on the future they will miss out on opportunities in the present. When they do think about their futures, I want them to have a sense that positive experiences await them. My children anticipate the future, but are not impatient to experience it now nor are they in a hurry to grow up.

I don't dwell on the future and the many responsibilities of adulthood in discussions with my children. I have tried hard to protect them from too many pressures and the demands that can occur with busy schedules and many activities outside the home. One of my greatest satisfactions is in knowing that I have been able to provide my children with the time to just be children. I hope they will some day look back and appreciate that they have had a true childhood that allowed them to be kids and to grow up as they were ready.

Still, I would be remiss in my parenting if I didn't help my children to understand that someday they will have more responsibilities and they need to develop good habits even now. My goal is for my children to grow to be independent adults, contributing to society and especially to those who are closest to them. In addition to teaching basic life skills, I talk to my children about the need to learn and develop themselves in ways that will help them in the future.

I thought that my occasional talks about the future had really made an impact on Josh, when we went to my nephew Jeff's high school graduation ceremony. I had talked to Josh about Jeff's many academic achievements, as well as the numerous musical and athletic accomplishments Jeff had attained during his high school years. Jeff was graduating at the top of his class, and I pointed out to Josh that it had taken a lot of hard work but Jeff was now being rewarded for his efforts.

Shortly before the graduation ceremony was to begin, we met Jeff and his parents inside his high school. Jeff was wearing the traditional cap and gown, and was surrounded by proud relatives and friends. As Jeff and his mother walked down the hallway to line up with the rest of the graduating class, Josh thoughtfully watched them go.

"Mom," he said. "Someday that's going to be me and you."

I can hardly describe how thrilled I was at this unexpected notion that Josh was actually considering his future. My emotions soared as I realized that Josh must finally understand the value of hard work and a good education. At last all of my exhortations to him were paying off! Surely Josh would be much more self-motivated during schoolwork times now that he had gained such valuable insight.

As I stood in the high school hallway next to Josh with a contented smile on my face, Josh continued on to say: "Yep. I'm gonna be a head taller than you just like Jeff is taller than his Mom." So much for the value of my little motivational chats with him! I obviously still have much work to do.

My older two children are now in their early teenage years. I enjoy them immensely, and I look forward to being with them as they navigate the remainder of their adolescent years and enter adulthood. I know there will be new and different issues to address as my children grow older. Their needs will change, and they will become more independent.

Regardless of the many changes we experience, some things need not change. I will continue to relate to my children with respect for who they are now and who they can become some day. I will try and make sure that they know they are loved, no matter what happens. The road ahead has many uncertainties, but my children will not walk that road alone. If I concentrate too much on the difficulties, I will lose out on the blessing of knowing and appreciating the unique children in my life.

I believe that I am giving my children a foundation that will equip them for life. Sometimes Beckie asks me question after question in order that she can one day explain things to her own children. This gives me hope that I am creating a home life that my children will desire to reproduce for their own children some day.

I am continuing on in my journey of parenting and homeschooling my children. It has not been an easy sojourn, but it has been deeply satisfying. I believe that my struggles and successes are not meant for my benefit alone, but to encourage and inspire others who are on journeys of their own. I know there are many other people with stories to tell, and when I hear them I am encouraged and motivated to persevere. It is a privilege to be able to share my own experiences in the hope of helping others. I will endeavor to continue sharing as I learn and grow throughout my life. May God richly bless you.

Melinda

Heads Up! Helping

Heads Up!
Helping All Kinds of Special Kids

~~~~~~~~~~~~~~~~~~~~~~~~~~~~~~~~~~~

Melinda L. Boring, MA-CCC/SLP

www.headsupnow.com

171

Bibliography and Recommended Reading

Andersen, Ole, Marcy Marsh & Dr. Arthur Harvey (1999). *Learn With The Classics.* California: LIND Institute.

Buzan, Tony (1974). *Use Both Sides Of Your Brain.* New York: E.P.Dutton.

Campbell, Don (2000). *The Mozart Effect For Children.* New York: HarperCollins Publishers, Inc.

Dennison, Paul E. & Gail E. Dennison (1994). *Brain Gym, Teacher's Edition Revised.* California: Edu-Kinesthetics, Inc.

Freed, Jeffrey & Laurie Parsons (1997). *Right-Brained Children In A Left-Brained World.* New York: Fireside Simon & Schuster Inc.

Gardner, Howard (1999). *Intelligence Reframed.* New York: Basic Books.

Hannaford, Carla (1995) *Smart Moves.* Virginia: Great Ocean Publishers.

Hopkin, H. & H. Smith (Eds.). (1993). *Willard and Spackman's Occupational Therapy, Eighth Edition.* Philadelphia: J. B. Lippincott Company.

Kranowitz, Carol Stock (1998). *The Out-of Sync Child.* New York: Skylight Press.

Maxwell-Hudson, Clare (1994). *Aromatherapy Massage.* New York: DK Publishing, Inc.

Sousa, David (2001). *How The Brain Learns: A Classroom Teacher's Guide.* California: Corwin Press, Inc.

Sunbeck, Deborah (1996). *Infinity Walk.* California: Jalmar Press.

Tobias, Cynthia Ulrich (1996). *Every Child Can Succeed.* Colorado: Focus on the Family Publishing.

Vitale, Barbara Meister (1982). *Unicorns Are Real.* California: Jalmar Press.